S0-DUW-124

The National
SHARK-O-PEDIA

Author's conception of "Megamouth's" profile. (See page 69)

The National
SHARK-O-PEDIA

A helpful and informative guide to the recognition and identification of many sharks occurring in American territorial waters, especially the waters of the Hawaiian Islands, eastern Gulf of Mexico, and the west coast of Florida.

Victor R. Faughnan

Fully illustrated with 40 photographs, drawings
and many additional inserts.
Honolulu, Hawaii

ABOUT THE COVER:

The cover photo is a composite, the underwater scene is from a photo by Bill Milisen; the large Mako shark is from a photo by the author.

The back cover photo is from the author's collection.

All the photographs and pen and ink drawings are by the author or from his personal collection, except where noted.

All specimens shown in the various figures are of Hawaiian species except where otherwise noted.

Library of Congress Cataloging in Publication Data

Faughnan, Victor R.
  The National SHARK-O-PEDIA

80-81115   8003   800305
ISBN 0-916630-11-0

Copyright © 1980

All rights reserved

First edition 1980

Published By:
    Undersea Resources, Ltd.
    P.O. Box 15844
    Honolulu, Hawaii 96815

Manufactured in USA

Designed by the Author

Dedication

Dedicated
to the
Memory
of
Captain John Kuahiwinui
A son of Hawaii, he fished Hawaiian waters for some thirty-five years. He was skillful in his profession and unselfish in sharing his knowledge with others. He left a legacy of fishing skills and fishing lore which will be used in Hawaii as long as boats and fishermen sail Hawaiian seas.

Mahalo and Aloha

13'8" gravid female (contained over 70 embryos) tiger shark, 1,086 pounds taken off Sand Island, Oahu, Hawaii, March 1980 by the author and Bill Babbitt. Photo by Stan Wright.

Insert: Bill Babbitt with the jaw from this specimen.

CONTENTS

Fig. 1. The author fishing in Hilo Bay, Hawaii aboard the research vessel "Machias", 1971. (Top shark is an 11' Tiger).

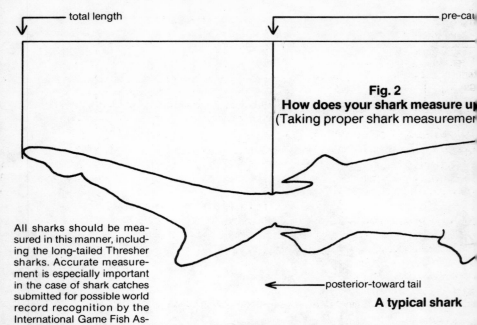

total length

pre-cau[dal]

**Fig. 2
How does your shark measure u[p]**
(Taking proper shark measuremen[t])

All sharks should be measured in this manner, including the long-tailed Thresher sharks. Accurate measurement is especially important in the case of shark catches submitted for possible world record recognition by the International Game Fish As-

posterior-toward tail

A typical shark

sociation. *Never* obtain the total or pre-caudal length by following the contour of the body.

With the shark laid over on its side, place one or more yardsticks end to end on a flat surface behind the shark. With a T-square line up the front edge of the first yardstick with the tip of the shark's snout. Without allowing the yardstick(s) to move, remove the T-square and again line it up with the tip of the tail. Now read the total length. Repeat the same procedure for the head and pre-caudal lengths.

PREFACE

The College edition of the New Webster's Dictionary says, "Shark, n. (origin uncertain) Any of a group of elongate, cartilaginous, mostly marine fishes, order Selachii, certain species of which are large and ferocious, destructive to other fish and to man".

These creatures are the subject of this book. In the pages that follow you will be provided with enough information on sharks to enable you to know and understand them better.

The main purpose of this volume is to aid the general public, fishermen (both commercial and sport), divers, students, shark enthusiasts and even marine biologists, in the identification and recognition of those sharks known, encountered or caught in their area. To facilitate instruction and training, a complete set of flash cards and slides is available from the publisher for a fee. Please write for further information.

The format chosen for this book is that of a textbook: it lends itself easily to the location of specific information on sharks. The user need simply go to the section in question without the necessity of reading unwanted text. Technical terms and words are kept to a minimum to facilitate use and understanding. The most technical aspect of the entire book is the use of scientific names of the various families, genera (genus) and species. For instance: CARCHARHINIDAE (The Gray Shark Family), *Carcharhinus* (one genus found in this family) and *obscurus* (species). The scientific name for the species usually will reflect an individual shark's most prominent or unusual

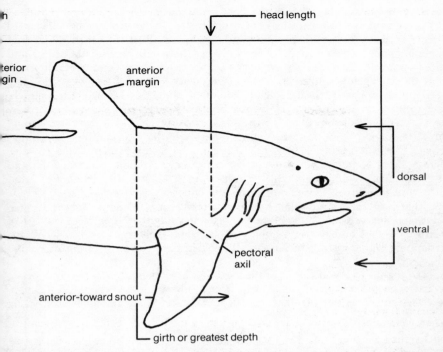

characteristic, habit or behavior; and in many cases the name of the species honors the individual first responsible for its identification.

The practice of assigning scientific names is important for at least two good reasons: first, to maintain some form of order throughout the scientific world; and second, because the people in various parts of the world tend to name sharks in their particular area after familiar objects, places, habits, local persons or even after local events. This latter practice results in what is referred to as the common name. As you may have guessed, because of this there are more common names of sharks then there are sharks. In the example given earlier for a scientific name *(Carcharhinus obscurus)*, the species name comes from the word obscure. Let's return to Mr. Webster's book, the dictionary: "obscure, a. Not easily understood; not expressed with clarity; not clear or distinct to any sense; removed or remote from worldly or important activities; unnoticed, or unknown to fame, etc." The intention of the individual who assigned this name *obscurus* was apparently to show the following: that a shark so abundant and so large as well as readily recognized by so many scientists throughout the world for so long, could have remained clouded in confusion many years before being accurately classified.

Much of the material throughout this book is firsthand, obtained by the author during numerous field cruises on the following programs: the "1967–1969 Cooperative Shark Research and Control Program" for the University of Hawaii under the direction of the late Dr. Albert L. Tester; the "1971 State Shark Control and Research Program" for the State of Hawaii, Department of Land and Natural Resources, Division of Fish and Game, under the combined direction of Mr. Kenji Ego, Mr. Henry Sakuda and Mr. Michael Fujimoto; and most recently on the "1976 Shark Utilization and Student Training Program" for the Department of Planning and Economic Development for the State of Hawaii. On these last two programs the author served as consultant, advisor and field investigator.

Not any one individual's knowledge of a subject such as *sharks* would be sufficient to complete such an undertaking without calling on the efforts of others. With that thought in mind, I would now like to acknowledge those individuals, publications and authors whose efforts and published works were so helpful in the ultimate completion of this book: Bigelow and Schroeder's classic work Fishes of the Western North Atlantic, Sharks Part I; Susumu Kato, Stewart Springer and Mary Wagner Field Guide to Eastern Pacific and Hawaiian Sharks; Sharks and Survival edited by Perry Gilbert, published by D.C. Heath and Co., Boston; Harold W. McCormick and Tom Allen with Capt. William E. Young Shadows In the Sea published by Chilton Books; Dr. Albert L. Tester 1967–1969 Cooperative Shark Research and Control Program Final Report, University of Hawaii; Henry Sakuda, Michael Fujimoto 1971 Shark Control and Research Program State of Hawaii, Department of Land and Natural Resources, Division of Fish and Game; Johnson T.F. Chen A Review of the Sharks of Taiwan published by Tunghai University, Taichung, Taiwan, China; Bigelow and Schroeder A Study of the Sharks of the Suborder Squaloidea Bulletin of the Museum of Comparative Zoology at Harvard College Vol. 117, No. 1; the International Game Fish Association, All Tackle Shark Records for both men and women.

Special thanks to the members of the local Shark Anglers Club of Largo, Florida, especially David Peterson, Dave Blanchard and John Campbell; also to Bill Greenway, owner and operator of The Indian Rocks Tackle Shop, Indian Rocks Beach, Florida. All of the above provided information on their shark catches, experiences and provided fresh specimens for the author's camera.

Correspondence concerning the information presented in this book can be addressed to the author in care of the publisher. Contributions of new information will be credited to the contributor in future additions of this work.

To the following individuals I wish to express my gratitude: Dr. Jack Randall of the Bernice P. Bishop Museum of Honolulu, Hawaii; Dr. Leighton Taylor, Director of the Waikiki Aquarium, Honolulu, Hawaii; Dr. Paul J. Struhsaker, and Mr. John J. Naughton, fishery biologists NOAA National Marine Fisheries Service, Honolulu, Hawaii; Dr. Richard C. Wass (formerly of the Dept. of Zoology, University of Hawaii) Marine Resources, Government of American Samoa, Pago Pago, American Samoa; Mr. Charles DeLuca, Curator of the Waikiki Aquarium, Honolulu, Hawaii; Mr. Robert Retherford, professional diver, underwater photographer, aqua culture consultant, author, and President of Undersea Resources, Ltd.; Mr. Spencer Wilke Tinker, former Director of the Waikiki Aquarium, Honolulu, Hawaii and author of Sharks and Rays, Fishes of Hawaii, Pacific Crustacea, and numerous other scientific and marine-oriented publications; Joyce Geyer, who contributed so much to the realization of this book.

To all of the above I am indebted for the assistance given me in the early days of the compilation of the material for this book.

At this time I would like to acknowledge Mr. Franklin Kang and Mr. Eugene "Gene-o" Platino, both of Honolulu, who over the years participated with me during many shark fishing endeavors either off Pier 7 in Honolulu Harbor or aboard my sampan. To both these gentlemen, a sincere thank you for their friendship and the sharing of our mutual interests together.

And finally to my son Mr. Robert M. Faughnan, who provided the final incentive I needed which he showed by his interest in the completion of this book: "thanks, pal".

"Basic Sharkology / Characteristics"

Sharks come in all shapes, sizes and forms, with outward body features that are diversified. Before one can attempt to identify any shark as to family or species, certain facts should be available. It is with this goal in mind that this publication is directed; to provide the facts necessary for individuals interested in shark identification.

Obviously, the first step in shark identification is to determine that the fish in front of you is, in fact, a shark. In order for a fish to qualify as a shark, certain external and internal features must be present. Regardless of what shape or profile they present, they are sharks, provided that five or more gill-slits are present on the sides of the head; a curved mouth is located on the underside of head area; the skeleton is of cartilage; with a slight layer of calcium (no true bone); dermal denticles (scales) cover the hide; pectoral fins are joined to the head at or behind the third gill-slit; fins are rigid, not compressable; and no air bladder is present.

Certain facts should be kept in mind when attempting to identify sharks. The body proportions, the fin size, location, and other features are somewhat inconsistent. Many of the body features and dimensions, as well as coloration, change with the shark's growth. Coloration is the least consistent for identification in most cases as coloration depends on environmental and dietary habits.

Due to these inconsistencies, slight variations in identifiable characteristics are often encountered. In most cases of close similarity of outward features, the teeth become an extremely important tool in the ultimate identification of any shark.

All sharks, regardless of sex, outwardly appear the same except for one difference; a male shark will have two horizontal appendages (cigar-shaped) attached to the pelvic fins, called claspers. These appendages in young immature males are semi-rigid. They become much more rigid in mature males due to both a cartilaginous interior and some calcification externally. During copulation the male releases sperm directly into the oviduct of the female through grooves on the inner sides of both claspers. It is not known with certainty whether the male inserts one or both claspers when mating; however, as the female possesses two individual uteri, it would suggest that both claspers would be inserted, assuring fertilization of both. Once inserted a sort of clasp folds out of each one. In this way the male is able to remain attached to the female, in addition to holding onto the dorsal fin of the female with its teeth.

To determine sex in a damaged specimen, when the pelvic fin area is missing, simply open the body. If female, you will find a uterus on both sides of the body cavity.

The claspers of male sharks may be useful in some cases for identification, or at least will aid by eliminating certain species. Suppose you see two young male Gray sharks (neither displays obvious markings) in front of you and both are five feet in length. You notice the claspers of one are much larger, more rigid, and perhaps slightly calcified indicating this shark is mature. The other shark has smaller claspers, less rigidity, and no apparent calcification; apparently an immature individual. In noting the obvious difference between the two, you have shown them to be separate species— *which* species, remains to be learned.

Now it is necessary to know the size at which different species reach maturity. For instance, some Gray sharks that reach maturity between four and five feet include, Sandbar, Small Black-Tipped and the Gray Reef.

A few Gray sharks not yet mature at five feet are the Galapagos, Silky, and the Bignosed. We can now assume that two of the species mentioned will fit our two specimens. In order to establish each one's true identity we must examine closely their body features. As neither shark displays obvious markings, we can eliminate both the

1

Small Black-Tipped and the Gray Reef. Thus the process of elimination has left you with one probability; the Sandbar shark: is most likely the identity of the mature specimen. As both the Silky and the Big-nosed can also be eliminated using known features. The Silky, has smaller, less-conspicuous dermal denticles. The Big-nosed, which as its name implies, has a moderately long snout. We again are left with one probability, the Galapagos shark, which is most likely the identity of the immature specimen.

The method discussed above is workable, but as it is only an example of one situation, it shouldn't be assumed it will work easily in all similar cases. In the situation above, one other feature could aid in the identification and/or elimination of the suspected species—the teeth.

Teeth—Their "Fingerprints"

The teeth of many sharks are very diagnostic, that is, some of them have uniquely-shaped teeth that are found only in their particular family or species. On the other hand, many species have similar teeth. This is very evident in the Gray Shark Family (CARCHARHINIDAE). This close similarity makes accurate identification to the species very difficult within this family. Many members of this group have broad triangular upper teeth (blade-like) with serrated edges and only slight differences in shape. In order to determine the species, it is necessary to closely examine body features. Problems with identification of members within this family are further multiplied as it is the largest family of sharks, including some fifteen genera (genus) and sixty species. Fortunately, several of these species have teeth that are very distinctive, which helps reduce the number of choices.

Once one becomes able to discern slight differences in the teeth, the job of identifying will be easier—not easy, just easier. No two species will have teeth exactly alike, similar yes, but like our fingerprints, their teeth possess their own distinct character.

The teeth of one shark may have smooth edges; another fine serrated edges; still another, large serrations. The teeth of one may be cylindrical; another may be triangular; still another may have narrowly triangular teeth. The central cusps may be

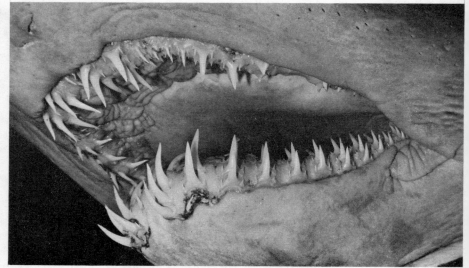

Fig. 3. 'Jaws', the teeth of *O. ferox*.

erect; others slightly oblique; still others may be strongly oblique. The base of the teeth may be notched on one or both sides; others may have secondary cusps on either side of the central cusps with or without notches. The teeth may have only one central cusp (uni-cuspid), two cusps (bi-cuspid), three cusps (tri-cuspid), or four, or more (multi-cuspid).

Most teeth will be designed for cutting (triangular with serrated edges), for ripping, tearing, and grasping (cylindrical), or for crushing (pavement or cobblestone like). The range is as varied and diversified as is the diet of sharks.

The teeth of the upper jaw are used for positive identification, as these differ from one species to another. The teeth of the lower jaw usually appear quite similar, especially in members of the Gray Shark Family—more precisely, individuals of the genus *Carcharhinus*. However, in some cases in which the upper teeth are very similar; the shape, the presence, or absence of serrated edges on the lower teeth could be a decisive factor in the final identification.

Sharks obviously are rough, coarse feeders. They violently grab their prey, viciously snap their jaws down, and swim off shaking their head from side to side. In this way they are capable of severing bones. One might ask, with this kind of table manners, how they are able to retain a mouth full of teeth? Surely they must break or lose many teeth. True, they frequently lose and break teeth; however nature endowed them with an enviable feature, that, if possible in humans, would place all dentists on unemployment. The teeth you see in the mouth of a shark are called functional teeth; usually one, sometimes two or three rows of functional teeth are in position and used for feeding. Unseen under gum tissue are several more rows. There are commonly five to seven rows of teeth, but a few species may contain up to fifteen or more. The teeth under the gum tissue are called replacement teeth. When a tooth is broken or lost, the next tooth in position behind it begins to move up and forward filling in the space left in the functional row. All other teeth in the same row progressively advance. At the bottom of the row a new tooth will begin to form, insuring the availability of teeth for as long as the shark lives. This progressive movement is much like a woman's hand fan when opened. Also, the tooth behind is slightly larger than the preceding teeth, thus allowing for the growth of the shark's body.

External Features of Sharks

The following list clearly shows diversity among the sharks of the world. It is these differences that ultimately determine the family, genus and even the species to which sharks are assigned. Scientists responsible for the classification and identification of marine life use these varied features to segregate, sort, organize, and in effect bring order and understanding to what otherwise would be mass confusion.

1. Most will have five gill-slits, while others will have six or even seven.
2. Some will be armed with dorsal spines; on most they are absent.
3. Some will have functional spiracles in addition to gills; on others, spiracles may be absent, non-functional, or present but very minute.
4. The caudal (tail) of most species will be asymmetrical (upper lobe longer than lower lobe), while in others they will be symmetrical (crescent-shaped, both lobes equal in length or nearly so). In some the lower lobe may be absent or nearly so.
5. Dorsal fins will vary in size, shape and location. First and second dorsal fins may be equal in size or nearly so. The second dorsal may be much smaller and even inconspicuous. The first dorsal may be well forward, well to the rear, or even absent.
6. The anal fin is present in most, while absent in others.
7. Pectoral fins may be short and wide, or may be long and slender.

8. Snouts will vary from short and blunt to long and pointed. Some may be narrow, others will be flattened, many will be rounded.

9. Some sharks will have a keel, others may have two, most have none.

10. A ridge may be present on the midline of the back, prominent on some, and weak or absent on others.

11. Some sharks will have barbles attached to the nostrils (like feelers), but barbles are absent on most.

12. Most sharks will display varying shades of gray for color, others may show pastel shades; some will have spots or stripes; others may have patterns; a few may exhibit luminescence.

13. Bodies may be long and slender, short and fat; others may be round or flattened.

14. Some sharks may be only inches in length and be fully mature; others will be immature giants of fourteen feet or more.

15. Hides will be covered with dermal denticles (teeth-like scales). Most will be inconspicuous to the eye. Some will be prominent. All will be apparent to the touch.

16. Some will possess, in addition to both an upper and lower eyelid, a third eyelid called nictitans (nictitating membrane). The latter is absent on many sharks.

The hide or skin of sharks is similar to that of man, because both possess two layers. The upper or surface layer is called the epidermis, which like man's, can regenerate itself. The second layer, the dermis, which is below the epidermis and protected, provides the pigmentation or coloration of the hide. The exposed outer layer is covered with placoid scales called dermal denticles. These denticulated scales are in reality thousands of minute teeth. The surface of these 'teeth' is composed of dentine. These scales, like the teeth in their mouths are the closest thing to bone in their entire body. These tiny scales, like true teeth, possess a root canal, blood vessels and nerves. The hides of all sharks have these toothy-scales. On most they are rather inconspicuous, but a few possess very prominent ones. Both the shape and the size of these denticulated scales vary from one species to another. Many will be so aligned as to overlap each other. Others will be spaced some distance apart. To some degree, the scales can be used for the identification of sharks. However, as their shape and appearance fluctuates somewhat from one area of the body to the other, this characteristic should be examined with caution. The presence of these dermal scales produces a rough sandpaper texture to the shark's skin which can be felt by running your hand along their bodies from the tail toward the head. Shark hide is very durable; so durable that it is used by commercial manufacturers in the production of shoes, belts, wallets, women's purses, and even leather two-piece dress suits. The average cowhide has a tensile strength rating of about 4,000 psi, whereas shark hide has a rating of about 7,000 psi. Only three shark tanneries have produced leather in recent times, I believe only two are presently in operation; one is located in Japan, the other is in New Jersey called "Ocean Leather". Of these two companies, "Ocean Leather" is said to produce the best quality leather. The main reason for their success apparently is due to their secret process used in the removal of the dermal denticles from the hide. The most desirable of all shark hides is that of the Tiger shark *Galeocerdo cuvier*. At one time "Ocean Leather" paid a premium for Tiger shark hides which had to be of good quality. These "quality" hides had to be free of all blemishes; no "skinner's marks" or mating scars could be present.

4

Some sharks possess one other somewhat specialized apparatus called "nictitans" or nictitating membrane. These nictitans are located immediately in front of the eyeball and below, (when not in use), and are concealed under the hide. Most sharks possess both an upper and a lower eyelid which have only a small amount of movement. The purpose of the nictitating membrane is to provide some added protection to the eyes during feeding as well as from any excessive amount of bright light. When the eyes are threatened by any object or strong light, this membrane will move upward from under the hide covering the entire eye. When the threat subsides the membrane will regress back to its original position. A captured shark may lay motionless for long periods, a good rule is to poke a stick gently near the eye; if alive this membrane will cover the eye; if dead, there will be no response. *Be sure your shark has these membranes.*

Important Internal Features

Sharks differ internally from the Teleosts, the true bony-fishes, as they possess neither a swim bladder (air bladder) or any true bone.

This swim bladder possessed by true bony fishes enables them to remain at any given depth without the necessity to swim. They are able to accomplish this by adjusting the amount of air within this bladder. A similar method is used by man to control the depth of a submarine which is accomplished by the increase or decrease of ballast which, in turn, regulates its weight versus buoyancy.

Sharks, on the other hand, not possessing this organ, are more dense (heavier) than the amount of water their bodies displace. Because of this, sharks are normally required to continually provide forward motion to avoid sinking to the bottom. There may be exceptions to this. The reader is referred to the text under the Sand shark *Odontaspis taurus* and this section under Respiration.

Perhaps the one singular characteristic which more than anything else separates all selachians (sharks), from the true fishes, is the skeleton. As with all Elasmobranchii, that is, the Orders of Selachii (sharks) and Batoidei (rays, skates and links), their skeletal frames lack any true bone cells. The skeletons are composed of a mixture which includes a cartilaginous substance with some calcification. As sharks never developed a swim bladder they must continually swim to maintain their equilibrium in the water (the reader is referred to pages 9–49). Because of the lack of this organ, the skeleton of cartilage instead of bone is beneficial to sharks as it is much less dense than true bone. Also the livers add buoyancy to their bodies due to the high oil content.

How are sharks, that are normally a saltwater animal, able to survive in fresh water? Many sharks are known to frequent brackish waters, water that is of both fresh and salt content, such as at mouths of rivers and areas where rivers empty into harbors. Of all the sharks that enter brackish water only one penetrates the barrier between brackish and fresh or sweet water regularly and for extended periods. That one shark is known throughout the world by many scientific names, and those are: *Carcharhinus leucus, C. nicaraguensis, C. zambezensis, C. gangeticus.* No doubt other names exist as well. Regardless of the names known to scientists, these sharks are all the Bull shark *C. leucus.*

The following scientific statement sheds some light on the physiology involved but as yet, science is unable to explain fully how the Bull shark and a few pelagic fishes manage to survive extended periods of time in the freshwater environment. Through the process of 'Osmosis' liquids and gases interchange through a membrane that separates them. In this case, two liquids (water containing different amounts of salt)

5

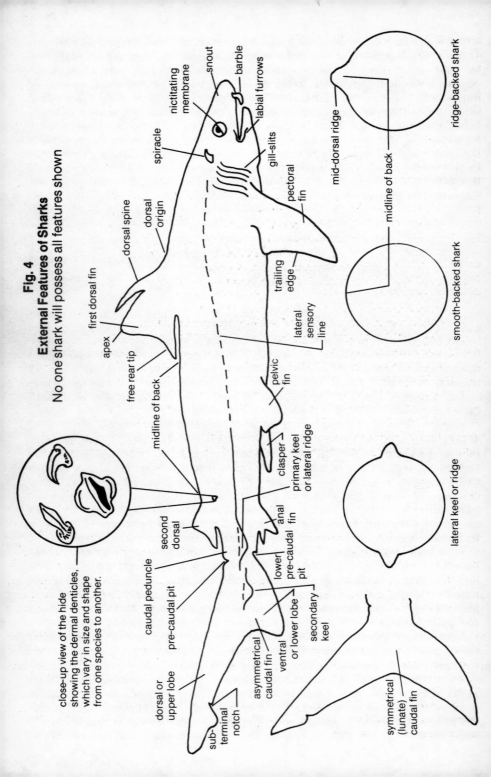

Fig. 4
External Features of Sharks
No one shark will possess all features shown

close-up view of the hide showing the dermal denticles, which vary in size and shape from one species to another.

snout
barble
nictitating membrane
labial furrows
spiracle
gill-slits
dorsal spine
dorsal origin
pectoral fin
first dorsal fin
trailing edge
apex
free rear tip
lateral sensory line
midline of back
pelvic fin
clasper
primary keel or lateral ridge
second dorsal
anal fin
lower pre-caudal pit
caudal peduncle
pre-caudal pit
asymmetrical caudal fin
ventral or lower lobe
secondary keel
dorsal or upper lobe
sub-terminal notch

mid-dorsal ridge
midline of back
ridge-backed shark
smooth-backed shark

lateral keel or ridge

symmetrical (lunate) caudal fin

are separated by a membrane (in the gills) which is more permeable to water than salt. This allows the water to pass from the weaker-solution to the stronger until both are equal.

True bony fishes (teleosts) release water from their bodies to the sea, their body fluids are less salty than seawater. Because of this they need to regenerate their body fluid which they do by taking in water and releasing salt to the sea.

Sharks, on the other hand, retain large amounts of urea (part of the composition of urine) in their blood stream and flesh. It is the presence of these waste products in the flesh that account for the strong odor so common with sharks. Along with this urea they also retain some trimethylamine oxide. Because of the presence of these two waste products the body fluid of sharks is somewhat saltier than seawater. Due to this condition sharks need not drink. What little water they require will enter through the permeable membranes located in their gills. As stated earlier this does not answer the question how Bull sharks are able to freely inhabit bodies of fresh water without becoming saturated with water.

It is my opinion that Bull sharks have become adapted through evolution for extended, but limited, excursions into fresh water. They may be able to tolerate several days or perhaps weeks in fresh water before the necessity to return to salt water compels them to do so.

Reproduction

The eggs of all female Carcharhinids (Gray sharks) are internally fertilized. This fertilization is always accomplished through intercourse by the insertion of the male's claspers (mentioned previously) into the cloaca (anal opening) of the female. In this manner the sperm is transferred.

The eggs of a female are produced in the ovary, each ovum or egg upon ripening begins to enlarge and becomes reddish-yellow along with the formation of a yolk. After a period of time, the egg will progress from the ovary and will ultimately arrive at either the left or right uterus, having received fertilization along the way. The egg is now covered with a thin membrane which will stretch and support the developing embryo. During this initial stage of development the embryo will be sustained by extracting nourishment from the bright yellow yolk to which it is attached. As the embryo consumes the yolk another process begins; a yolk sac placenta is formed which attaches to the uterine wall and then is connected to the developing embryo via an umbilical cord. In this manner allowance is made for the further nourishment and the removal of waste products through the mother.

The elapsed time required from conception to birth (gestation period) is approximately 12 months (for most Carcharhinids). The pupping season occurs in the summer months; July, August, and September. This is supported by the capture of many females with expanded, enlarged and stretched uteri in late summer and fall. It is possible that the pupping season may be different among the numerous species of this group of sharks. Likewise the gestation period may vary as well.

The entire reproductive period (fecundity)—the cycle from the initial conception to the final release of the embryos, the birth, and the reconception—is about two years.

For an actual eyewitness account of a gravid (pregnant) female Sandbar shark *(Carcharhinus milberti)* giving birth in captivity, the reader is referred to page 64. "Field Observations".

The embryonic development cycle discussed above is found among those sharks referred to as "viviparous", by which method the majority of sharks accomplish the replenishment of their kind.

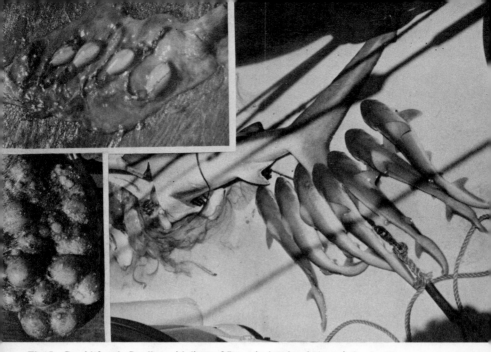

Fig. 5. Gravid female Sandbar with litter of 7 terminal embryo's (puppies).
Inserts: (upper) 4 egg yolks developing in the uterus, (lower) an ovary showing large ripening eggs. (Note: umbilical cords and placenta visible from body cavity.)

There are two additional embryonic reproductive methods known; the second most common is called "ovoviviparous". As with viviparous embryos these are likewise developed within the mother; however, these embryos will have no direct connection with the mother; a shell forms around the embryos which later breaks (the young hatch within the mother). At this point the young continue to develop within the uterus in a free state receiving nourishment through secretions deposited in the uterus by the mother.

The third method of embryonic formation is "oviparous", which is the least common among sharks. Initially the embryos of these sharks develop in the same manner as the viviparous and the ovoviviparous sharks. With oviparous sharks the embryos are also fertilized within the mother. They too begin development within an egg case; however, these egg cases are not retained but are released by the mother and deposited on the sea bottom where they become attached with sticky tendrils to coral, rocks, seaweed or some other suitable surface. Here they remain attached, developing until they hatch.

Respiration

The breathing process of sharks is not unlike that of man. As a shark swims, its mouth is opened to allow water to enter. The throat at this time is blocked off by the contraction of muscular tissue (similar to feeding). In this manner the incoming water is forced to exit through the various gill-slits or clefts. As the water rushes through the gills, oxygen is extracted and absorbed into the blood. Simultaneously carbon dioxide is released from the blood into the water. This transfer of oxygen and carbon dioxide is accomplished by the presence of gill-filaments located in each gill-slit or cleft which contain numerous blood vessels.

When a shark inhales water these slits or clefts are closed. This allows the water to pass over the gill-filaments. At this point the release of carbon dioxide occurs and the oxygen present in the water is absorbed.

Many sharks also possess a pair of organs called spiracles. These spiracles are located behind either eye. These interesting organs are part of the respiratory system though their exact function is somewhat speculative. They are thought to assist the gill-slits in the aeration of the blood assuring a good supply of oxygen to both the brain and the eyes. As mentioned earlier, some sharks have large conspicuous spiracles which are obviously functional (e.g., False Cat shark). Others possess very small inconspicuous spiracles (e.g., Whale sharks and many *Carcharhinids*), which are so minute as to suggest they are non-functional. It may be that the more modern sharks *(Carcharhinids)* only possess a remnant form of spiracles which through evolution are gradually disappearing.

Most species of sharks breathe by continually swimming in order to provide a constant flow of water across their gill-filaments. This requirement for perpetual swimming may be interrupted occasionally. For instance a sick or extremely tired individual is capable of temporarily lying on the bottom and while motionless will flex its gill-slits. This interlude will last perhaps no more than fifteen or twenty minutes, at which time the shark must begin swimming again in order to increase the quantity of oxygen into its bloodstream.

The author feels that some sharks which frequent deeper water well off shore may be capable of a similar behavior. As they would be unable to reach the bottom, they may simply place themselves in a swiftly moving current. Facing this current with their mouths open, they may in effect be able to "hover", allowing the swift current to flush their gills. It could be that sharks use such a behavior to rest or sleep, or at least reduce their bodies' rate of metabolism.

A few species are known that are capable of voluntarily flexing their gill-slits indefinitely. These sharks are often observed lying motionless on the bottom in caves, among rocks, as well as in the open. In fact, it may be that they will only swim to forage for food, search out a mate, or when threatened by man or some other predator.

The preceeding pages are intended to provide the reader with a deeper knowledge into the general characteristics, that together with the physical features combine to produce the somewhat familiar profiles we know as "sharks". Hopefully, the information given in this section will make the reader become more observant in any future contact with sharks.

The intention of this book is to provide you, the reader, with an insight into the realm of sharks and shark identification. This book contains much of the necessary information. All you need is the interest, some initiative, and a desire to answer the question—"What kind of shark is that?".

1-1 Oceanic White-Tipped Shark
Pterolamiops (Carcharhinus) longimanus (Poey), 1861
Also known as White-Tip shark

Most prominent feature   Apex of first dorsal fin is broadly rounded and most fins are mottled or white-tipped.

Fig. 6. Oceanic White-Tipped Shark
Inserts: (left to right) Close-up of upper jaw; Complete jaw.

Color   Various shades of gray, light-gray, grayish-brown, to grayish-blue above; undersides white to dirty-white.

Size   Maximum lengths of about twelve feet suggested for this species, though most individuals are seven to nine. Maturity is reached at about seven feet in length. Fully grown adults may exceed several hundred pounds in total weight.

Reproduction   Fertilization is internal, gravid females capable of at least six embryos in a litter. Young are born alive and free swimming.

Diet   Most likely includes much of the readily available marine life in open ocean waters, such as, both large and small fishes, whales and perhaps even sea-turtles.

Range   Almost entirely pelagic: an open ocean, blue-water shark which is observed in great abundance. Rarely enters inshore waters; at least no such occurrence is recorded. Found in most of the warmer waters of the world's oceans.

Danger rating   A very dangerous, reputed man-eater; one of the most abundant sharks observed at the scene of air and sea disasters. Displays an aggressive and curious nature when confronted.

Economic importance   Often responsible for damage to both the catch and gear of commercial fishermen. Not recognized by the International Game Fish Association as a game fish.

Related species   Uncertain, it is possible that variations of this species may occur.

Physical features peculiar to this species
1. Most fin tips white or dirty white, often mottled.
2. First dorsal fin with rounded apex.
3. Second dorsal and anal fin usually conspicuously black (not white-tipped).
4. Origin of first dorsal fin behind pectoral fin trailing edge.
5. Snout rounded as viewed from above.
6. Caudal fin is assymmetrical in shape.
7. Pectoral fins are long, wide, with rounded tips.
8. A mid-dorsal ridge will be present on some, weak or absent on many.

1-2 Great Blue Shark
Prionace glauca (Linnaeus), 1758
Also known as Blue Whaler, Blue shark

Most prominent feature   Long slender body (see color below).

Color   Various shades of blue, indigo-blue, bright-blue above, clean white undersides.

Size   Is recorded as reaching lengths of twenty feet but seven to nine is more common. Maturity reached at about seven to eight feet. Adults may exceed four hundred pounds in weight (computed for total length of twelve feet).

Reproduction   Fertilization is internal, a prolific species, gravid females contain up to fifty or more embryos in a litter. Young are born alive and free swimming measuring twelve to eighteen inches in length.

Diet   Will feed on most available marine life; such as, various open ocean schooling fishes both large and small, whales, squids, and other sharks.

Fig. 7.   Great Blue Shark—With portion of litter delivered during capture.*
Inserts: (left to right) Close-up of upper jaw; Complete jaw.

11

Range A pelagic species; almost entirely an open ocean, blue-water shark, occurring in large schools and/or congregations. Infrequently found in shallow coastal waters other than as strays or disoriented individuals. Occurs in most of the warmer waters of the world's oceans.

Danger rating Very dangerous, implicated in several recorded attacks on both man and boats.

Economic importance Considered by many to be an active game fish when caught on rod and reel. Causes considerable damage to both the gear and catch of commercial fishermen. This species is recognized by the International Game Fish Association as a game fish.**

Related species None.

Physical features peculiar to this species
1. Body long and slender.
2. Pectoral fins are long and narrow.
3. Eyes are moderately large.
4. Snout is long and pointed.
5. First dorsal fin is about midway between the pectoral fins and pelvic fins.
6. Caudal fin is asymmetrical in shape.
7. There is no ridge present on midline of the back.
8. The eyes possess a nictitating membrane, there are no spiracles present.

*The embryos shown in fig. 7 were released prematurely after capture and represent only a portion of the litter, some nineteen were observed expelled. All were alive and active, several were placed in large plastic bags filled with salt water. About four hours later they were placed in a large holding tank on shore; none survived.

**The present world record for this shark is a tie between Mr. Richard C. Webster and Mrs. Martha C. Webster; both were caught at Rockport, Mass., both were taken on 80 pound test line, Mr. R.C. Webster's Great Blue weighed 410 pounds, its length was 11′6″, its girth was 4′4″, and it was caught on 1 Sep 1960; Mrs. M.C. Webster's Great Blue also weighed 410 pounds, its length was 11′2″, and its girth was 4′4½″ and it was caught on 17 Aug 1967.

1-3 Sandbar Shark
Carcharhinus milberti (Muller and Henle), 1841
Also known as Brown, New York Ground shark

Most prominent features High erect first dorsal fin, with its origin well forward of pectoral fin trailing edge.

Color Various shades of gray, brownish-gray to slate-gray, even brown above, undersides white.

Size Recorded as reaching lengths of seven to eight feet; most individuals being five to six feet. Seldom mature at less than five feet. Weights exceeding two hundred pounds are uncommon for this species. Gravid females usually are heavier than the males. Specimens taken off the eastern seaboard, including Florida, tend to reach 7½ feet in length and Hawaiian Sandbars tend to be slightly smaller.

Reproduction Fertilization is internal. Gravid females contain two to thirteen embryos in a litter with eight being common. Gestation period is about thirteen months. The young are born alive and free swimming. Newly born pups are eighteen to twenty-two inches in length. (Refer to "Field Observations").

Range Primarily littoral (frequents inshore waters, enters bays and harbors). Commonly found in depths up to three hundred feet (50 fathoms), with some occurring in

Fig. 8. Sandbar Shark
Inserts: (left to right) Close-up of upper jaw; Complete jaw.

deeper water at times. Often seen with back and first dorsal fin out of the water when crossing shallow sandbars, hence the name "Sandbar". Occurs from New England to South America, Gulf of Mexico, Hawaiian Islands, and no doubt elsewhere in the Pacific; however, the Hawaiian Islands is their only known occurrence in the central Pacific.*

Diet   Prefers small fish a foot or less in length, includes crustacea (crabs, lobsters, etc.), as well as eels and octopus. Will readily prey on various locally available marine life including various rays. Some stomach contents revealed small sharks; perhaps new born pups. Seldom includes man's trash and garbage in its diet.

Danger rating   Never implicated in any confirmed fatal attacks on man; however, due to its size, dentures, and abundance should be considered dangerous especially in dirty, murky water.

Economic importance   Considered a valuable food fish, its flesh known to be very tasty. It is a nuisance to fishermen, by damaging commercial fishing gear, such as nets, longlines and handlines. The skin is used for leather and the liver for vitamin-A. Not recognized by the International Game Fish Association as a game fish.

Related species   None.** Sometimes confused with the Galapagos shark *(C.*

*It is quite possible that a population of Sandbar sharks is also present throughout the "Line Islands". This is based on a conversation between the author and Mr. Robert A. Retherford, who has frequently dived in the area, especially at Palmyra Island.
**One species, described as a close relative of the Sandbar shark by two American scientists, Theodore Gill and J. F. Bransford in 1877, was the Bull shark *C. leucus* (see Dusky shark, related species). This shark does closely resemble the Sandbar in profile. They both display a prominent, high and erect first dorsal fin, which on both is located well forward of the pectoral fins' posterior margins, about over the axil of the pectoral fins. The only noticeable difference between the two species as seen by a diver would be in the shape of the first dorsal fin; that of the Bull is somewhat shorter, its anterior margin is more inclined from the perpendicular toward the apex; its posterior margin is vertical toward the free rear tip. Due to the more inclined margin of its first dorsal it suggests a broad-sail, much more so than the Sandbar. Captured specimens of the two species can readily be separated: the Sandbar is a ridge-backed shark; whereas, the Bull is a smooth-backed shark (no mid-dorsal ridge).

13

galapagensis), separable from this species by the higher and more erect first dorsal fin; body margin from snout to origin of first dorsal fin is more immediately vertical as compared to the more rounded margin of *C. galapagensis.* Another species that could be confused with *C. milberti* is the Big-nosed shark *(C. altimus),* however, the teeth of *C. altimus* are so distinctive in shape they easily separate the two species. At least one other Gray shark, the Dusky *(C. obscurus),* might be easily confused with the Sandbar. It is readily distinguished from the Sandbar by its smaller and further back first dorsal fin. Another noticeable difference is to be found by comparing the undersides of both sharks which on the Dusky shark is grayish, as are the fintips. This coloration is the characteristic from which the name "Dusky" is derived.

Physical features peculiar to this species
1. The first dorsal fin is prominently high and erect.
2. A prominent medial or mid-dorsal ridge is present on the midline of the back between both dorsal fins.
3. The caudal fin is asymmetrical in shape.
4. The snout is broadly rounded as seen from above.
5. Often some fins may show white trailing edges; not *white-tipped.*
6. The body is rather heavy. It presents a pudgy appearance.
7. The first dorsal fin's origin is about over the axil of the pectoral fins (well inside of the trailing edge).
8. The eyes possess a nictitating membrane. There are no spiracles present.

1-4 Galapagos Shark
Carcharhinus galapagensis (Snodgrass and Heller), 1905
Also known as Gray shark

Most prominent feature　High erect first dorsal fin, its leading edge nearly straight,

Fig. 9. Galapagos Shark
Inserts: (left to right) Close-up of upper jaw; Complete jaw.

with its origin slightly behind pectoral fin trailing edge, (differs from *C. milberti* in this respect).

Color   Various shades of gray, slate-gray, dark-gray with one specimen being emerald green above; underside white.

Size   Recorded as reaching lengths up to twelve feet; most individuals seven to nine feet. Attains maturity at six to seven feet. Adults may weigh three hundred pounds or more. Smaller individuals of this species tend to be less heavy-bodied than the "pudgy" Sandbar *C. milberti*.

Reproduction   Fertilization is internal. Gravid females may contain six to sixteen embryos in a litter; nine being common. Gestation period about twelve months. The young are born alive and free swimming and are about fifteen to twenty inches in length.

Diet   Feeds on various locally available marine life such as small and large fishes, squids, octopus, crustacea (crabs, lobsters etc.), rays, and other sharks. The Galapagos shark also will consume man's garbage and trash as many stomach examinations have shown.

Range   Being littoral, it frequents inshore waters; occurring commonly in depths of fifteen to twenty-five fathoms (90 to 150 feet). Will feed at all depths, bottom, midwater as well as the surface, occurs more often around islands throughout the Pacific. May be found far offshore as well.

Danger rating   Very dangerous; a reputed man-eater. Large individuals are capable of inflicting serious injury or death.

Economic importance   Numbers are insufficient to support any commercial market, however, it is edible. No doubt responsible for some damage to commercial fishing gear. Not recognized by the International Game Fish Association as a game fish.

Related species   None. Smaller individuals often confused with the more common Sandbar shark *(C. milberti)*. Galapagos sharks are separable from the Sandbar sharks by their generally larger size and broader bodies. Also, the body margins of *C. galapagensis* from snout to the origin of the first dorsal fin are more rounded, not as immediately vertical as displayed by the Sandbar (see Sandbar shark, Related species).

Physical features peculiar to this species
1. The origin of the first dorsal fin is well behind the pectoral fins' trailing edge.
2. A well-formed mid-dorsal ridge is present on the midline of the back between both dorsal fins.
3. The snout is narrowly rounded as seen from above.
4. The caudal fin is asymmetrical in shape.
5. The teeth are broadly triangular with moderately large serrated edges.
6. The eyes possess a nictitating membrane. There are no spiracles present.

1-5 Tiger Shark
Galeocerdo cuvier (Peron and LeSueur), 1822
Also known as Leopard shark

Most prominent feature   Body marked with dark vertical blotches or bars (stripes) from gill area to upper lobe of caudal fin. Very prominent in young; weak or absent on large adults.

Color Gray to grayish-brown above; upper portion of body is usually darker than sides, with white undersides

Size Reported to reach lengths of thirty feet; such lengths remain to be authenticated. Known to attain lengths of twelve to fourteen feet with authenticated lengths of fifteen to eighteen. Adults capable of weights in excess of 1,500 pounds. Maturity attained between ten to eleven feet, though gravid females from twelve to thirteen feet are more common.

Fig. 10. Tiger Shark—Taken aboard the research vessel "Easy Rider" during the "1976 Shark Utilization and Student Training Program", off the Hawaiian Islands.

Inserts: (left to right) Close-up of the teeth; Jaw of 7'1" Small Black-Tipped, Jaw of a 15'1" Tiger, Jaw of a 10'1" Galapagos shark; Close-up showing the rows of replacement teeth.

Reproduction Fertilization is internal, a prolific shark; females capable of bearing large litters or broods of up to fifty or more embryos. One specimen recorded contained eighty-two embryos. Gestation period of two years is likely. The young, born alive and free-swimming, are about twenty-four inches in length.

Range Both pelagic and littoral: occurs far out at sea as well as inshore. When in close proximity to land, enters shallow inshore waters at night. Commonly enters shallow bays and harbors; frequents river mouths as well. Occurs in depths of ninety to one hundred and eighty feet regularly; however, will be found both shallower and deeper. Seems to prefer shallow waters during nighttime hours; appears to return to open-ocean and deeper water in daylight hours. Known to occur in most warm waters throughout the world; eastern United States, Florida, Gulf of Mexico, and throughout the Pacific Ocean. A very common shark off the Hawaiian Islands.

Diet Apparently prefers slow-swimming marine life such as puffer fish and sea turtles. Definitely a feeder of opportunity; will readily sample as food simply anything that presents itself. The stomachs of specimens examined contained the following items: other sharks—whole or parts, various fishes—large and small, sea turtles, porpoise, portions of whales, cats, dogs, cattle, sheep, rats, birds, chickens, horses, sea

16

lions, rays, as well as remains of human beings. Tigers consume an endless list of trash and garbage; wire, tin cans, paper, plastic, wood, nails, rocks (coral), clothing, fishing gear, and other paraphernalia. In short, it is a scavenger in the truest sense of the word.

Danger rating   Highly dangerous, a reputed man-eater; will sample man with little or no hesitation. Capable of dismembering a man of considerable girth easily. A sluggish swimming shark when not feeding, but once excited by the scent of food or the erratic behavior of wounded fish it becomes very fast and aggressive. This species is guilty of a great number of attacks on humans throughout the warmer waters of the world.

Economic importance   The flesh of young Tiger sharks is used as food; however, larger Tigers are not considered desirable. Hide is used commercially for leather; and is considered the most desirable of leathers. Liver was used at one time for extracting vitamin A. The jaw is capable of producing some one hundred teeth sometimes used in making unique jewelry. Recognized by the International Game Fish Association as a game fish. The present record on rod and reel for a Tiger shark is: 1,780 pounds; its length was 13 ft. 10½ in. with a girth of 8 ft. 7 in.. It was caught at Cherry Grove, South Carolina on June 14, 1964 by Walter Maxwell on 130 pound test line.

Related species   None. Very unlikely to be confused with any other shark. This species was formerly known as *Galeocerdo cuvieri*. This shark is in no way related to the Leopard shark *Triakis semifasciata,* a common California species. Along the coastal waters of India this shark is known by the scientific name of *Galeocerdo rayneri.*

Physical features peculiar to this species
1. The body is marked with dark vertical blotches or bars (stripes) from gill area to upper lobe of caudal fin.
2. The snout is short, wide and prominently blunt as seen from above.
3. A prominent mid-dorsal ridge is present on the midline of the back between both dorsal fins.
4. A well-pronounced primary keel is present on both sides of the peduncle.
5. The caudal fin is asymmetrical in shape.
6. A well-developed lip or groove is present on underside of the snout.
7. A small, inconspicuous spiracle-slit is present behind both eyes.
8. The teeth are unique, cocks-comb in shape; the central cusp is triangular with large serrations and notched on one side with large serrations.
9. The eyes possess a well-developed nictitating membrane.

1-6 Gray Reef Shark
Carcharhinus amblyrhynchus (Bleeker), 1856
Also known as Gray Reef Black-Tipped shark

Most prominent feature   Wide, dark band on caudal fin from lower lobe upward along trailing edge to terminal notch.

Color   Various shades of gray, dark gray, bluish-gray above; undersides are white.

Size   Attains a length of eight feet although most are smaller. Reaches maturity at about four and a half feet in length and may exceed one hundred pounds in weight.

Reproduction   Fertilization is internal. Gravid females will contain from three to six embryos in a litter. Gestation period about twelve months. Young, born alive and free-swimming, are eighteen to twenty-two inches in length.

Fig. 11. Gray Reef Shark
Inserts: (left to right) Complete jaw; Close-up of upper jaw.

Diet Readily feeds on various reef fishes both large and small; the list may include eels, octopus, some crustacea (crabs, lobsters, etc.), and various schooling fishes in open water.

Range A littoral species: frequents inshore waters; common near reefs, and seems to prefer clean, clear waters of atolls and smaller Islands. Most often found in abundance around small, less-populated or polluted Islands; large, densely populated Islands have few or none. Waters high in oxygen content may be requirement of this species. Common in depths of fifteen to twenty-five fathoms (90 to 150 feet). Occurs in fair numbers off some of the Hawaiian Islands.

Danger rating This species has been guilty of provoked and unprovoked attacks on man and areas where they are abundant should be avoided. A very fast and agile species with a territorial and curious nature; when excited it becomes quite aggressive. This species, when in distress, displays a "threat-posture" which can be recognized by the arching of its body and the pointing of the pectoral fins downward. This action is like that which some dogs display toward an unwanted stranger: if the dog's threat is ignored, an attack is invited. If this sort of display takes place while you are near these sharks, discontinue your activity and leave the area.

Economic importance None. Not recognized by the International Game Fish Association as a game fish.

Related species This species was formerly known as *Carcharhinus menisorrah* (Muller and Henle), 1841. At least one other species may be identical to *C. amblyrhynchus,* the Island shark *C. nesiotes.*

Physical features peculiar to this species
1. A wide dark band on trailing edge of caudal fin.
2. Most fin tip areas are darker than body color (not black-tipped).
3. Caudal fin is asymmetrical in shape.

18

4. Weakly developed ridge on midline of back (between first and second dorsal fins).
5. First dorsal fin origin well behind pectoral fin trailing edge.
6. Snout rounded as viewed from above.
7. The eyes possess a nictitating membrane, there are no spiracles present.

1-7 Small Black-Tipped Shark
Carcharhinus limbatus (Muller and Henle), 1841
Also known as Black-Tip, Spot-Fin, Carconetta, Spinner shark

Most prominent feature   All fins are conspicuously black-tipped, the lower lobe of
he caudal fin being most prominent. A dark band runs along both sides of the body.

ig. 12.   Small Black-Tipped Shark
Inserts: (upper and lower left) Complete jaw, upper jaw of Small Black-Tipped Shark; (upper and
lower right) Complete jaw, upper jaw of Large Black-Tipped Shark.

Color   Various shades of gray to dark gray, dusky, even blue-gray above; undersides
are white. The prominent black-tips of the fins in younger individuals may fade with
growth.

Size   Total lengths of up to eight feet are attained; although most individuals are five
to seven feet. This species matures at four to five feet. Adults reach weights exceeding
one hundred pounds.

Reproduction   Fertilization is internal. Gravid females contain two to nine em-
bryos in a litter with four to six common.

Diet   Individuals frequenting shallower inshore waters feed on fishes both large and
small as well as squids, octopus, and eels. The pelagic members no doubt have a
similar diet. Schools of Small Black-Tipped sharks follow commercial fishing boats at
sea feeding on the scrap fish thrown overboard. It is assumed that their diet includes
stingrays; captured black-tipped sharks often have stingray barbs protruding from
the jaw and gum tissue.

19

Range   Both pelagic and littoral: occurs commonly in large schools far out at sea as well as inshore in fair numbers. One specimen, a pup, (umbilical scar still visible) was caught by the author in a shallow harbor of the Big Island (Hawaii). This species frequents the inshore coastal waters of many areas in fair numbers. It is commonly found in water depths ranging from fifteen to twenty-five fathoms (90 to 150 feet). This shark is known throughout the warmer waters of the world, from New England to Florida; in the Caribbean and South America; in the eastern Pacific from California to Peru; and in the central Pacific off the Hawaiian Islands.

Danger rating   This shark is suspected of unprovoked attacks on man; however, there appear to be no authenticated accounts on record. Due to its size, dentures, abundance, and its very fast active swimming nature, it is considered potentially dangerous. The author has been told by many scuba-divers of their encounters with this very aggressive and determined shark during several dives while spearing octopus and other fish. For an account of one such incident, the reader is referred to "Field Observations".

Economic importance   At one time, due to the abundance of this species, many shark fisheries utilized their hides for the manufacture of leather products. This species is not recognized as a game fish by the International Game Fish Association.

Related species   One, the Large Black-Tipped shark *Carcharhinus maculipinnis* this differs from *C. limbatus* in having longer gill-slits, smaller eyes, and smooth edges to the lower teeth. The Large Black-Tipped shark and its smaller cousin are so alike in appearance that they are often confused with each other and are frequently misidentified. For an account of this type of identity problem, the reader is referred to "Field Observations". In many areas of the world these two species are known by the common name "Spinner Shark", and are named this because they both display the same behavior of leaping from the sea, spinning their bodies in midair and falling back to the surface.

Physical features peculiar to this species
1. All fins are conspicuously black-tipped (prominent on smaller individuals, faded or absent on some larger ones).
2. A dark band of upper body color extends backward on both sides, and the white color of the underside extends forward and above it.
3. The snout is narrowly pointed as seen from above.
4. The caudal fin is asymmetrical in shape.
5. There is no mid-dorsal ridge present on the midline of the back between the dorsal fins.
6. Both an upper and a lower precaudal pit are present above and below the peduncle
7. The second dorsal fin originates almost directly over the anal fins origin.
8. The edges of the teeth in the lower jaw are serrated.
9. The eyes possess a nictitating membrane, there are no spiracles present.

1-8 Black-Tipped Reef Shark
Carcharhinus melanopterus (Quoy and Gaimard), 1824
Also known as Reef Black-Tipped shark

Most prominent feature   The tips of all fins are ink-black, the middle third of the first dorsal fin is a lighter shade of the darker body color.

Color   Various shades of brown coffee-cream brown, dark brown, above; under sides are white. A dark band of upper body color extends backward on both sides

Fig. 13. Black-Tipped Reef Shark
Inserts: (left to right) Complete jaw; Close-up of upper jaw.

and a band of white of the underside extends forward and above it.*

Size Lengths of six feet are common; large individuals of ten feet have been reported, although this size is questionable. Maturity is reached at about four to five feet. Adults may exceed one hundred pounds in weight.

Reproduction Fertilization is internal. Gravid females may bear less than a dozen embryos in a litter. The gestation period seems to be about twelve months. The young are born alive and free-swimming and are about twelve to fourteen inches in length.

Diet Consists of various smaller reef fishes, including, eels, squids, octopus, and crustacea (crabs, lobsters etc.).

Range A littoral species which congregates inshore on or near shallow reefs; no doubt enters deeper water in its search for food. A fairly well-known shark throughout the lower Islands and atolls of the central Pacific. Once known to be an abundant species around the Hawaiian Islands; now very sparse in distribution, especially around the more populated major Islands. The waning population may be due to the increase of pollution and use of the inshore coastal waters by man.

Danger rating Young individuals display a somewhat shy and timid behavior coupled with a curious nature. Despite their apparent docile character, at least one unprovoked attack on man is recorded.

Economic importance None. Not recognized by the International Game Fish Association as a game fish.

Related species None. Easily distinguished from all other black-tipped sharks.

*The specimen shown in fig. 13 was frozen and frosted over, due to this the dark band on the side of the body is absent.

Physical features peculiar to this species

1. The tips of all fins are conspicuously ink-black.
2. A dark band of upper body color extends backward on both sides and a band of white on the underside extends forward and above it.
3. The snout is blunt and rounded as seen from above.
4. Caudal fin is asymmetrical.
5. The first dorsal fin origin is even with or slightly behind the pectoral fin's trailing edge.
6. There is no ridge present on the midline of the back.
7. The caudal fin's leading and trailing edges have heavy ink-black margins.
8. The eyes possess a nictitating membrane, there are no spiracles present.

1-9 Big-nosed Shark
Carcharhinus altimus (Springer), 1950
Also known as Knopp's shark

Most prominent feature   The distance from the tip of the snout to the mouth is usually greater than the width of the mouth; however, this is somewhat variable changing with growth and is most notable in younger individuals. The teeth are easily identified because they remain unchanged with growth.

Color   Various shades of gray, brown to copper above; undersides are white.

Size   Recorded as attaining lengths of ten feet; although, most are five to seven feet. Maturity is reached at about five to six feet. Fully grown adults may exceed two hundred pounds in weight.

Reproduction.   Fertilization is internal. The young are born alive and free-

Fig. 14. Big-nosed Shark
Inserts: (left to right) Complete jaw; Close-up of upper jaw. Photo by John Naughton. Insert photos by the author.

swimming. Knowledge of this species' breeding habits is still lacking; litters of seven or more embryos likely.

Diet   Probably samples much of the locally available marine life. The shape and size of the teeth suggests that both large and small fishes are its prey.

Range   This species appears to be more littoral than pelagic: seems to prefer the deeper waters over the continental slopes. Occurs more often in water fifty fathoms (300 feet) or deeper. Some individuals enter the shallower coastal waters at night foraging for food on the surface. Known to occur in the western Atlantic, Florida Keys and Hawaiian Islands.

Danger rating   Due to its normal deepwater habits this shark is considered no threat to man. However, because of their potential large size and teeth and the fact that they are found in shallow waters at night, if encountered it could be dangerous to man.

Economic importance   None. Not recognized by the International Game Fish Association as a game fish.

Related species   None. Due to the similar body features, this species could easily be confused with several other Gray sharks especially the Sandbar *(C. milberti)* and the Galapagos *(C. galapagensis)*. The Sandbar shark is perhaps the closest in similarity; both these sharks have very high and erect first dorsal fins. The Galapagos shark is similar with a moderately high and erect first dorsal fin and is large and heavy-bodied like the Big-nosed. The Sandbar shark can be further separated from the other two because it seldom exceeds seven feet in length and has a smaller body girth. The long snout of the Big-nosed shark *(C. altimus)* is not as pronounced in adults and the teeth can be used to distinguish it from the Sandbar, the Galapagos shark, or any Gray shark, as they are quite different.

Physical features peculiar to this species
1. The snout length (from mouth to tip of snout) is usually greater than the width of the mouth (more pronounced in young individuals).
2. The nostrils have finger-like lobes (nasal flaps).
3. The snout is rounded as seen from above (may be slightly pointed).
4. A prominent mid-dorsal ridge is present on the midline of the back.
5. The origin of the first dorsal fin is at or behind the pectoral fins trailing edge.
6. The caudal fin (tail) is asymmetrical in shape.
7. The eyes possess a nictitating membrane, there are no spiracles present.

1-10 Dusky Shark
Carcharhinus obscurus (LeSueur), 1818
Also known as
Shovelnose, Dusky Ground shark

Most prominent feature   The snout is short and blunt (see related species).

Color   Various shades of gray, bluish to leaden above. Undersides are white except the pectoral fins; the tips of which are sooty or dusky (hence the name).

Size   Adults may attain twelve to thirteen feet in length; although most will be ten feet or less and weigh several hundred pounds. Maturity is reached at about seven feet in length.

Fig. 15. Dusky Shark—Shark angler John Campbell shown with his catch (12-11-76) on Big Indian Rocks Pier, Indian Rocks Beach, Florida.

Inserts: (upper) Close-up of upper jaw; (lower) Complete jaw.

Reproduction   Fertilization is internal. Gravid females may produce up to fifteen or more embryos in a litter. The young are born alive and free-swimming.

Diet   Will feed on most locally available marine life as do other sharks its size and genus.

Range   Mostly littoral; however, individuals do occur in open ocean far from shore. Frequents the shallow coastal waters inshore in many areas. A seasonal visitor from Massachusetts to Florida, and southern California to the Gulf of California. Its presence is suspected off the Hawaiian Islands.

Danger rating   Very dangerous, considered in some areas to be a harmless shark, by the uninformed.

Economic importance   Of some interest to shark fishing enthusiasts, who use rod and reel from boats, piers and shoreline. The teeth may be used for the manufacture of unique jewelry. Not recognized by the International Game Fish Association as a game fish.

Related species   None. This species is often confused with several other Gray sharks. The Dusky shark is distinguished from the Sandbar *(C. milberti)* by both the smaller size and the location of its first dorsal fin. The Bull shark *C. leucus,** also

24

known as the Cub or Ground shark, and the Lake Nicaragua shark *C. nicaraguensis* all differ from *C. obscurus* as they have no mid-dorsal ridge. The much shorter snout of the Dusky easily separates it from the Big-nosed shark *(C. altimus).* The Dusky shark is often confused with the more familiar Galapagos shark. The two can be separated easily, as the Dusky has a much shorter and more blunt snout compared to the longer and more rounded snout of the Galapagos shark. One other Gray shark often confused with the Dusky is the Silky shark *(C. falciformis).* The Silky differs from the Dusky with its longer, more broadly pointed snout; longer free rear tips of the anal, second dorsal fins; and larger and more diagnostic teeth as well as the smoother hide (due to smaller dermal denticles).

Physical features peculiar to this species
1. The snout is short and blunt.
2. The origin of the first dorsal fin is behind the pectoral fins trailing edge.
3. The caudal fin (tail) is asymmetrical in shape.
4. The undersides of the pectoral fins tips are sooty or dusky.
5. A mid-dorsal ridge is prominent on the midline of the back.
6. The eyes possess a nictitating membrane, and no spiracles are present.

*The Bull or Cub shark *C. leucus* mentioned earlier is worthy of further mention. It is a moderately large shark (8 to 10 feet) and very dangerous. This species, more than any other, frequents freshwater lakes and rivers that are navigable from the sea. In American waters the Bull shark is known to occur along the eastern seaboard including Florida, and is found in the Atchafalaya river of Louisiana and the Pascagoula river of Mississippi. There is little doubt that this shark *(C. leucus)* is the same shark that inhabits the Zambezi River of Africa and is known as the Zambezi River shark *(C. zambezensis);* in India's Ganges River as the Ganges River shark *(C. gangeticus)* and is also synonymous with *C. leucus.* Name a river or lake that empties into the sea and Bull sharks are known to be present offshore; then you should assume they are in that river or lake.

1-11 Silky Shark
Carcharhinus falciformis (Muller and Henle), 1841
Also known as Sickle shark

Most prominent feature   The anterior edge of the first dorsal fin is prominently inclined toward the rear. The free rear tips of both the second dorsal and the anal fins nearly reach the origin of the caudal fin.

Color   Shades of gray, dark gray, brown, even black above. Undersides are white.

Size   Fully grown individuals may attain ten feet in length. Most observed are six to eight feet. Most will be mature between five and seven feet. Adults will exceed two hundred pounds in weight.

Reproduction   Fertilization is internal. Gestation period, number of embryos and size at birth is uncertain. The young are born alive and free-swimming.

Diet   Will include much of the locally available marine life, such as various small fishes, squids and skates. The shape and size of the teeth suggests diet may include larger fishes and rays.

Range   An offshore pelagic species, found in fairly large numbers far out at sea. Many individuals enter the continental shelf coastal waters. A few may enter the shallower inshore waters while chasing or following schools of fish. Occurs off the Atlantic east coast, off California, and around the Hawaiian Islands in the central Pacific; no doubt in most warmer waters of the world.

Danger rating   Has never been directly implicated in attacks on man; however, due to its size, teeth and abundance offshore, this shark could be very dangerous.

Fig. 16. Silky Shark
Inserts: (left to right) Complete jaw; Close-up of upper jaw.

Unfortunately, when sea and air disasters take place the survivors are few, and those who do survive are unable to say if a Silky was among the marauders.

Economic importance   Probably considered a nuisance fish by commercial fishermen, damaging their catch, nets and other gear. Not recognized by the International Game Fish Association as a game fish.

Related species   As many as seven different species described, all with only slight differences. Of these, only two had been widely accepted; *Carcharhinus falciformis* in the Pacific and *Carcharhinus floridanus* represented in the Atlantic. Just recently the two species have been reclassified. It is now generally accepted that both are the same species, and *Carcharhinus falciformis* has become the singular generic representative of the two.

Physical features peculiar to this species
1. A long, narrowly rounded, nearly pointed snout, as seen from above.
2. The first dorsal fin origin is behind the trailing edge of the pectoral fins, and its anterior edge is strongly inclined toward the rear.
3. The dermal denticles (scales) are quite small (hide smoother to touch than most sharks).
4. The second dorsal and anal fin have longer free rear tips than most sharks, which nearly reach to the caudal fins origin.
5. A prominent mid-dorsal ridge is present on the midline of the back.
6. The caudal fin is asymmetrical in shape.
7. The eyes possess a nictitating membrane; there are no spiracles present.

1-12 Black-nosed Shark
Carcharhinus acronotus (Poey), 1861
Also known as Wreck shark

Most prominent feature The tip of the snout is sooty, dusky, or black in color (see related species).

Fig. 17. Black-nosed Shark (Florida specimen)
Inserts: (left to right) Close-up of upper jaw; Complete jaw.

Color Various shades of gray, yellowish-gray, cream-colored, and brown above. The undersides are white or weaker shades of the upper body. The snout tip is black or dusky; more noticeable in younger individuals.

Size A relatively small shark, seldom exceeding five or six feet in total length. This species is capable of reproduction at about three to four feet.

Reproduction Fertilization is internal. Gravid females will produce six or less embryos in a litter. The young are born alive and free-swimming at about seventeen to eighteen inches in length.

Diet Its feeding habits are uncertain; no doubt samples various small fishes, squids, and other smaller, bottom, dwelling marine life. This species is often included in the diets of larger sharks.

Range This species appears to be entirely littoral. It frequents very shallow inshore waters. In the western coastal waters off Florida this species occurs in fairly large numbers around sunken wrecks. Due to this, Floridians assigned it the obvious name "The Wreck Shark". Appears to be predominately associated with the Caribbean, Florida and the West Indies. Its center of abundance occurs off North Carolina, Gulf of Mexico, as well as South America.

Danger rating As these sharks congregate in fairly large numbers in shallow water they could represent a threat to anyone swimming or diving in their presence.

Economic importance Of little or no value commercially and may be considered a nuisance fish to shrimp, net, and handline fishermen. Not recognized by the International Game Fish Association as a game fish.

Related species There are none known to be related; however, a few species are very similar and often are confused with this shark. Two species often confused with the Black-nosed shark are the Small Tail shark *(Carcharhinus porosus)* and the Sharp-nosed shark *(Rhizoprionodon terrae-novae)*. Both of these sharks differ from the Black-nosed shark by the location of their second dorsal fin. Its origin is well behind the origin of the anal fin (see Fig. 19); whereas the Black-nosed shark has both the second dorsal and anal fin origins directly above and below each other.

Physical features peculiar to this species
1. The second dorsal fin origin is directly above the origin of the anal fin.
2. The snout tip is sooty, dusky, or black.
3. The snout is broadly rounded as seen from above, and relatively long.
4. There is no mid-dorsal ridge present on the midline of the back.
5. The teeth of the upper jaw are triangular, with a notch on one side. The serrations become much more coarse toward their base than along the central cusp, and the teeth become increasingly oblique toward the rear.
6. The eyes possess a nictitating membrane. There are no spiracles present.

1-13 Lemon Shark
Negaprion brevirostris (Poey), 1868

Most prominent feature Both dorsal fins are large and triangular; the second is nearly as large as the first.

Color The upper body is yellowish-brown, and sometimes dark brown to bluish-gray. The sides are yellowish. The undersides are often white to yellowish or olive gray.

Fig. 18. Lemon Shark (Florida specimen)
Inserts: (left to right) Close-up of upper jaw; Complete jaw.

28

Size May easily attain total lengths of eleven feet, but most are seven to ten feet. This species matures at about seven feet. Fully grown adults may exceed 300 pounds in weight.

Reproduction Fertilization is internal. Gravid females will produce several puppies in each litter (exact number uncertain). The young are born alive and free-swimming, and are about twenty inches in length.

Diet It may very well be an indiscriminate feeder. Its teeth suggest a varied diet of large and small fishes, octopus, and eels. Also, many are observed with stingray barbs in and about their mouths.

Range This species is entirely littoral: occurs in shallow coastal waters, enters harbors and dock areas, often found in both brackish and fresh water streams, creeks and river mouths. This species is known along the eastern United States from at least Massachusetts to Florida. Its center of abundance appears to be the coastal waters of Florida, Gulf of Mexico. It is not known in the central Pacific.

Danger rating In some areas where its presence is known, it has an almost docile reputation. Elsewhere it may be considered a man-eater. As with any shark that exceeds six feet in length it should be considered dangerous. Certainly its size and the abundance of jagged teeth should warrant one's caution and respect.

Economic importance In the past its hide was used for leather products, the liver for oil and vitamin A, and the fins were processed for use in shark-fin soup. Almost certainly, due to its shallow water habits, it causes some damage and inconveniences to commercial fishermen. Not recognized by the International Game Fish Association as a game fish.

Related species As many as six species have been described, however, they may be just slight variations of the same shark. One species known to occur off southern California, Sea of Cortez and Baja California, appears to be the same, *Negaprion fronto*. Its common name in Spanish is "Tiburon Amarillo" which means, Yellow Shark.

Physical features peculiar to this species

1. Both dorsal fins are large and triangular. The second is nearly as large as the first (separable from most carcharhinids in this respect).
2. The snout is short, very rounded, almost blunt, as seen from above.
3. The body generally displays a yellow or yellowish pigmentation.
4. The teeth are diagnostic, narrowly-triangular, erect and smooth-edged.
5. The eyes possess a nictitating membrane. There are no spiracles present.

1-14 Small Tail Shark
Carcharhinus porosus (Ranzani), 1839
Also known as Cuero duro shark

Most prominent feature The origin of the second dorsal fin is well behind the origin of the anal fin, and is about over the center.

Color Often described as leaden to bluish-gray on upper portions but is paler below. The margins or trailing edges of the lower fins often are white. Some black is often present on the rear margin of second dorsal. The several Florida specimens examined by the author were all generally a weak, pale yellowish-gray over the entire body. Because of this yellowish-gray appearance they are referred to locally (at Clearwater Florida) as "baby Lemon sharks".

Fig. 19. Small Tail Shark (Florida specimen)
  Inserts: Second dorsal fin origin behind origin of anal fin.

Size This species will seldom exceed four feet in total length. Most individuals are usually about three feet. Fully grown adults will not reach any great size or weight. Most will be less than thirty pounds or so.

Reproduction Unfortunately, very little is known pertaining to the sexual development of this species. Based on its relatively small size, individuals will be mature at about two feet in length. The eggs of females are fertilized internally, and the young are born free-swimming.

Diet It will readily feed on various small fishes, shrimp, squids, and the teeth shape suggest it may on occasion include small rays as its prey.

Range Appears to be an entirely littoral species and is seldom encountered more than a mile or so offshore. It is certainly a relatively common shark in the eastern Gulf of Mexico as shown by its occurrence in the continental shelf waters of western Florida. This small shark is probably subtropical; occurring in many coastal areas where moderately warm water is found. There are no reports of it from the central Pacific.

Danger rating As this shark may occur in some abundance in shallow water it could represent a potential threat to man. If excited by the presence of speared fish, a group of these small sharks could injure a diver seriously. At the present time, however, the author is not aware of any authenticated attacks on man by this species.

Economic importance In some areas of the world it is considered palatable and sold at fish markets. Where it occurs in any abundance it would likely be considered as a nuisance fish for entering fish traps, or taking baited hooks intended for more desired fish.

Related species None known. This species may easily be confused with three other sharks; *Carcharhinus acronotus* the Black-nosed, and two closely related species, *Rhizoprionodon terrae-novae* the Atlantic Sharp-nosed and its Pacific representative the Pacific Sharp-nosed shark *R. longuiro*. The Black-nosed shark differs from *C.*

porosus as its second dorsal fin origin is directly above the origin of the anal fin. Separating the two Sharp-nosed species from *C. porosus* is a little more difficult as all three have the same relationship concerning the location of the second dorsal and anal fins. The characteristics that help to distinguish *C. porosus* from the latter two species are: the small, almost inconspicuous labial grooves or furrows at the corners of the mouth and the small, inconspicuous nostril flap. Whereas, on both species of the Sharp-nosed sharks these two features are very prominent; very long, well-developed labial grooves or furrows and a longer, well-developed nasal flap.

Physical features peculiar to this species

1. The origin of the second dorsal fin is well behind the origin of the anal fin.
2. There are no spiracles present behind the eyes.
3. The notch at the terminal end of the caudal fins' upper lobe is relatively small (hence its name).
4. The eyes possess a nictitating membrane.

1-15 Sharp-nosed Shark
Rhizoprionodon terrae-novae (Richardson), 1836
Also known as Atlantic Sharp-nosed shark

Most prominent feature The corners of the mouth have long well-developed labial grooves or furrows.

Color The upper body varies from brown to olive-gray, the undersides are white. The margins or trailing edges of the pectoral fins are often without pigmentation, appearing clear, or white. The second dorsal and the lower lobe of the caudal fin are prominently black, as are the leading and trailing edges of both dorsal fins, and both lobes of the caudal fin.

Size A relatively small and slender shark which will seldom exceed three-and-a-half feet in total length. It is unlikely any fully grown individuals will surpass twenty pounds in weight, most will be perhaps ten pounds or less.

Reproduction The eggs of females are fertilized internally, and a litter of up to a dozen embryos may develop. After a gestation period of some twelve months the young are born alive and free swimming. This species attains sexual maturity between twenty-six to thirty inches in length. It has been suggested terminal embryos are ten to fifteen inches long; eight to twelve inches would be more likely. Initially the developing embryos are enclosed in weak shell casings within the uterine walls which later develop into a yolk-sac and placental connection to the mother.

Diet This small shark includes much of the available marine life found in its area as prey; such as, small fishes (parrotfish, and menhaden etc.), mollusks, shrimps, squids, etc. It may on occasion include small rays, crabs, and perhaps eels. Due to its somewhat small size it may, itself, be preyed upon by larger sharks.

Range This small shark appears to be entirely littoral in distribution. Occurs in considerable abundance in the shallow inshore coastal waters throughout the eastern and western Atlantic. It is known from as far north as Massachusetts, southward to the Florida Keys and into the Gulf of Mexico. It is somewhat numerous from southern Florida and along the eastern Gulf coast of Florida as well. It does not appear to occur in the Pacific region, however, a very similar species does (see Related species).

Danger rating As with most smaller species of sharks, only a minimal threat to man is likely. Individually it would be unlikely to confront a man, however a large

Fig. 20. Sharp-nosed Shark (Florida specimen): Note prominent nasal flap and the forward location of anal fins origin in relation to second dorsal.

concentration, excited by the spearing of fish or the presence of some other attractant would be a different matter.

Economic importance   This shark is often used as a source of protein in South America, and the West Indies and no doubt elsewhere. As this shark readily takes a baited hook, some commercial fishermen consider it a nuisance fish. In areas where it is openly accepted as a food source the shark would represent a marketable product, these fishermen would see it as a desirable fish.

Related species   One known, the Pacific Sharp-nosed *R. longurio,* the main characteristic that separates the two is based on the shape of the snout. The existence of the two species is questionable, they may well be one singular species with the difference in the snout being due to some developmental or inter-breeding transformation. For the present, the two species are classified by some as two distinct species, and by others as one species with two types; type one, the longer narrowly pointed snout, and type two, the shorter broadly rounded snout. The short snouted variety is the more common of the two. The genus *Rhizoprionodon* was formerly known under the genus *Scoliodon.* This shark could be confused with the Small Tail shark *Carcharhinus porosus,* however, the latter's teeth are dissimilar in shape, as compared to *R. terrae-novae's* which are similar in both jaws.

Physical features peculiar to this species
 1. The corners of the mouth have long well-developed labial grooves or furrows.
 2. The second dorsal fin originates over the mid-point of the anal fin's base.
 3. There is no mid-dorsal ridge present (smooth-backed) on the medial or midline of the back between the dorsal fins.
 4. The first dorsal fin origin is close to the pectoral fins trailing edge or slightly inside it.
 5. The nostrils have a relatively long and well developed nasal flap.
 6. There are no spiracles present behind the eyes.

7. The teeth are similar in shape, both jaws; the narrowly triangular central cusp is very obliquely inclined toward the rear, the edges are without serrations (only slightly wavy), and a notch is present on one side.
8. The snout is relatively short and broadly rounded as seen from above.
9. The eyes possess a nictitating membrane.
10. Both an upper and lower precaudal pit are present.

1-16 White-Tipped Reef Shark
Triaenodon obesus (Ruppell), 1835
Also known as White-Tip shark, Houndshark

Most prominent feature   Both dorsal fins and the upper lobe of the caudal fin are conspicuously white-tipped; the first dorsal and upper caudal fin are most prominent.

Color   Various shades of gray, slate-gray, to dark gray above; the undersides fade to white. Often the body is sparsely covered with dark spots or blotches along either side.

Fig. 21.   White-Tipped Reef Shark—Photo by Bill Milisen (Wake Island specimen).
Inserts: (left to right) Complete jaw; Close-up of upper jaw. Insert photos by the author.

Size   Lengths of seven to eight feet are not uncommon for this species. Maturity is reached at four to five feet. Fully grown adults may exceed one hundred pounds in weight.

Reproduction   Fertilization is internal; small broods of perhaps eight or less likely. The young are born alive and free swimming. The gestation period is about ten to twelve months.

Diet   Its haunts are both the bottom and inshore reefs, which suggest a varied diet; large and small reef fishes, eels, octopus, crustacea (crabs, lobsters, etc.), as well as some rays.

Range   This species is entirely littoral, it frequents the shallow inshore waters, preferring rocky bottoms. Often found lying inactive on the bottom (unlike most sharks, this one need not swim continually to breathe; it flexes its gills voluntarily to pump water through them) among rocks, crevices or even in caves. Known throughout the Indo-Pacific; often found around the Galapagos Islands, the Hawaiian Islands and elsewhere in the Pacific Ocean. May not be an inhabitant of the continental shelf of large land masses, at least not in any abundance.

Danger rating   As with most docile natured sharks, it is considered by many to be harmless. This shark, as with most animals, will, when threatened or provoked, defend itself. Due to both its size and sharp spike-like teeth, swimmers and divers should refrain from molesting it. One other word of caution; the liver of this species is said to be toxic and therefore should not be consumed by humans.

Economic importance   None. May be considered by many inshore fishermen to be a nuisance fish damaging hand-lines, traps, and nets. Not recognized by the International Game Fish Association as a game fish.

Related species   None. This species is normally found in the family Triakidae, however as most of its features are consistent with members of the family Carcharhinidae (except for its tri-cuspid teeth with two or more functional rows) it is treated here as a Carcharhinid shark. Three other sharks displaying white-tips are known; the Oceanic White-Tipped *(Pterolamiops longimanus),* the Silver-Tipped shark *(Carcharhinus albimarginatus),* and the Inshore White-Tipped shark *(C. platyrinchus).* All four of these species should be easily distinguished apart by their individual characteristics.

Physical features peculiar to this species

1. Both the dorsal fins and the upper lobe of the caudal have white tips (the white of the second dorsal often faded, inconspicuous, even absent).
2. The snout is short and blunt as well as somewhat depressed.
3. The nostrils have prominent flaps.
4. The second dorsal fin is about half the size of the first.
5. The sides of the body are sparsely covered with dark spots or blotches.
6. The caudal fin is asymmetrical in shape.
7. The eyes possess a nictitating membrane, and spiracles are present behind the eyes.

Family SPHYRINIDAE—2

2-1 Scalloped Hammerhead Shark
Sphyrna lewini (Cuvier, Griffith, and Smith), 1834
Also known as
Common Hammerhead, Mallet-Head, Hammerhead shark

Most prominent feature   A flattened, laterally expanded head, its leading edge is convex (curved backward) with four distinct lobes; the two central lobes produce an indentation in the center of the midline.

Color   Various shades of gray, light-gray, gray-brown, coffee-cream brown and beige above; the undersides are paler shades of above, or white.

Size   Known to reach fifteen feet in length, most are seven to ten feet. Maturity is attained at about seven to eight feet. Fully grown adults will exceed three hundred pounds in weight.

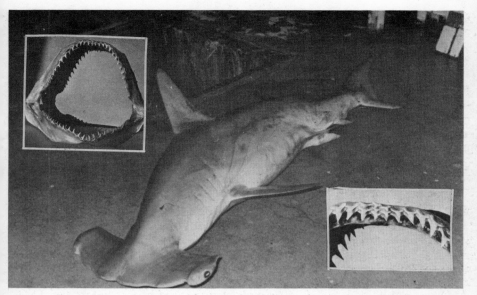

Fig. 22. Scalloped Hammerhead Shark—7′6″ taken off Oahu, Hawaii near Honolulu Harbor entrance. Inserts: (upper) Complete jaw; (lower) Close-up of upper jaw.

Reproduction   Fertilization is internal, a prolific species, gravid females are capable of bearing up to thirty or more puppies. The gestation period is most likely about twelve months.

Diet   Seems to prefer rays, stingrays, eagle-rays etc., also includes both large and small fishes, other sharks, eels, octopus, as well as crustacea (crabs, lobsters etc.). Some stomach examinations have shown that occasionally it will include man's garbage and trash.

Range   Both pelagic and littoral; found far out at sea, as well as inshore. There is some indication that the larger adult individuals tend to be pelagic, while the puppies and adolescents are more littoral. Gravid females commonly enter bays and harbors to bring forth their young in shallow protected waters. This species seems to have two major areas (that are known) for bringing forth their young (pupping); these areas are known as nurseries. One of these nurseries is located in the Atlantic in the vicinity of Long Island, the other is in the Hawaiian Islands. Occurs in the Atlantic from New Jersey to South America, southern California to South America, Indo-Pacific, and is very common in the central Pacific, especially off the Hawaiian Islands.

Danger rating   There have been several attacks on man attributed to this group of sharks. It has been difficult to place the blame accurately to the particular species involved. Of some seven known species in this family, three are suspect; the Scalloped Hammerhead *(S. lewini)*, the Smooth Hammerhead *(S. zygaena)*, and the Great Hammerhead *(S. mokarran)*. These three are most likely the dangerous ones, due to their potential sizes of thirteen to twenty feet in length; all other members seldom exceed six feet.

Economic importance   The larger individuals at one time were used commercially for moderate yields of vitamin A as well as for leather products. In some areas the flesh is considered tasty and sold on the market. Causes considerable destruction to commercial fishing gear. This species is recognized by the International Game Fish Association as a game fish. The IGFA apparently doesn't distinguish between the three largest species of this family. They simply accept the Hammerhead shark for world record competition. The present world record on rod and reel for a Hammerhead shark is 703 pounds, its length was 14 ft. 4 in., and a girth of 5 ft. 3 in., it was caught at Jacksonville, Florida in 1975 by H. B. Reasor.

Related species   At least six species are known, three of which are shown here; the Great Hammerhead shark *(Sphyrna mokarran),* the Bonnet-Head shark *(Sphyrna tiburo),* and the Smooth Hammerhead shark *(Sphyrna zygaena),* the latter species *S. zygaena* (not covered in the text) differs from the other two generally in head shape. The leading edge of the head has only three lobes on the midline which causes the absence of an indentation at the center of the midline (refer to the text for comparison).

Physical features peculiar to this species
1. The head is flattened and expanded laterally.
2. The head is convex (curved backward), the leading edge has four distinct lobes.
3. An indentation is present at the center of the midline.
4. The anal fin origin is forward of the second dorsal fin origin.
5. The first dorsal fin is broad.
6. The caudal fin (tail) is asymmetrical in shape.
7. The first dorsal fin is at, or slightly forward of pectoral fin trailing edge.
8. The eyes possess a nictitating membrane, there are no spiracles present.

2-2 Great Hammerhead Shark
Sphyrna mokarran (Valenciennes), 1822
Also known as Hammerhead shark

Most prominent feature   Head flattened and expanded laterally, its leading edge straight with four distinct lobes with an indentation at the center.

Color   Upper body is dark olive with undersides paler, even white.

Size   This species is the largest member of the family; lengths of eighteen to twenty feet are not uncommon. Sexual maturity is reached after about nine to ten feet of growth. Fully grown adults will reach several hundred pounds in weight.

Reproduction   Fertilization is internal, a prolific species; gravid females are capable of up to thirty or more puppies per litter. The young are no larger than 15 to 20 inches at birth. The heads of the new-born are curved at birth, becoming straight with growth. Because of this, very young specimens could be confused with the Scalloped Hammerhead *S. lewini.*

Diet   Prefers rays, stingrays, eagle-rays, fishes both large and small, and may include other sharks, eels, octopus and various forms of crustacea (crabs, lobsters etc.). Will sample man's garbage and trash occasionally.

Range   Both pelagic and littoral, found far out at sea as well as inshore. Occurs in most oceans of the world. Commonly found in shallow Florida waters. As yet no occurrence verified in the Hawaiian Islands.

Danger rating   Considered very dangerous, at least the larger individuals. It is difficult to place the blame in most cases of attacks. Of some seven known species, three are suspect or proven to being man-eaters, Scalloped, Smooth, and Great

Fig. 23. Great Hammerhead Shark—10′ caught by the charter boat "Lucky Lady" Clearwater Municipal Marina, Clearwater, Florida 1976.

Inserts: (upper) Complete jaw; (lower, left to right) Underside of head, close-up of upper jaw.

Hammerhead. These three are suspect due to their potential size of thirteen to twenty feet.

Economic importance   Larger individuals at one time were sought commercially for their livers as they had a high yield of vitamin A. Their hides were taken for leather products. In some areas their flesh is considered tasty and sold commercially. Causes some destruction to commercial fishing gear. This species is recognized by the International Game Fish Association as a game fish (see Scalloped Hammerhead).

Related species   At least six, three of which are shown; Smooth Hammerhead *(Sphyrna zygaena),* Scalloped Hammerhead *(Sphyrna lêwini),* Bonnet *(Sphyrna tiburo),* all differ mainly in shape of the head. All Hammerhead sharks have the general appearance of members of the family CARCHARHINIDAE differing only by the bizarre head shape.

Physical features peculiar to this species

1. The first dorsal fin is extremely high and erect, also quite narrow (nearly sickle-shaped).
2. The head is flattened and expanded laterally.
3. The leading edge of the head is straight, not curved (the head of the newborn is slightly curved, changing with growth); four distinct lobes are present.
4. An indentation is present at the center of the heads' leading edge.
5. The anal fin origin is forward of the second dorsal fin origin.
6. The caudal fin (tail) is asymmetrical in shape.
7. The first dorsal fin's origin is at, or slightly forward of, the pectoral fin's trailing edge.
8. The eyes possess a nictitating membrane, there are no spiracles present.

2-3 Bonnet Shark
Sphyrna tiburo (Linnaeus), 1758
Also known as Bonnet-Head,
Shovel-nose and Shovel Head shark

Most prominent feature Absence of the typical hammer-shaped head; which is more spade or shovel-like in appearance, noticeably curved. The leading edge has no lobes or indentation on the midline.

Fig. 24. Bonnet Shark—About 3′ taken off Big Indian Rocks Pier, Indian Rocks Beach, Florida 1976. Inserts: (upper left to right) Underside of head, pelvic fin with large claspers; (lower) Top view of body.

Color Various shades of gray to grayish-brown above; undersides are paler shades of upper-body color. Some individuals may show some small, dark, round spots on their sides.

Size A few individuals may attain lengths of six feet; however, most are five feet or less.

Reproduction Fertilization is internal, gravid females produce about nine puppies per litter. The embryos are first formed in an egg-like container and later emerge and become attached to the uterine wall by an umbilical cord within a yolk-sac placenta.

Diet Prefers crustacea (crabs, shrimp etc.), octopus, small fishes, larger individuals may include various rays.

Range Being littoral, it occurs almost entirely in shallow inshore waters of bays and harbors. Occurs from New England to South America in the Atlantic; in the Pacific it is observed off southern California to South America. A common inhabitant of both the Gulf of Mexico and Florida coastal waters.

Danger rating Considered to be relatively harmless, larger individuals could inflict some injury.

Economic importance Of little or no commercial value at the present time. May be used as a source of protein in some areas of the world. Not recognized by the International Game Fish Association as a game fish.

Related species Some six other species comprise this family of sharks. Refer to the text concerning other members of this family.

Physical features peculiar to this species
1. The head is spade or shovel-shaped (not hammer-shaped).
Note. Except for the head shape it has the general characteristics of all Hammer-head sharks.
2. The eyes possess a nictitating membrane, there are no spiracles present.

Family ISURIDAE—3

3-1 Great White Shark
Carcharodon carcharias (Linnaeus), 1758
Also known as
White, White-Death, Killer,
Man-Eater, White-Pointer, Blue-Pointer shark

Most prominent feature The caudal fin is symmetrical (crescent-shaped), the snout is conical (anvil-shaped).

Color This species usually has dark shades of black, gray, gray-brown or even slate-blue above; the undersides are white or oyster-white. Often a black circular spot is present near the axil or base of each pectoral fin. Many common names of this shark tend to suggest it is white; the reference to white refers more to its undersides and because some appear leaden-gray.

Size Extreme lengths have been reported over the years for this species, such as forty feet. One specimen was recorded as thirty-six and a half feet, it had been caught about one hundred years ago in Australia; at least a newspaper article about the catch gave its length as 36 feet 6 inches. The jaw had been removed and is now on exhibit at the British Museum. Dr. Jack Randall, a well-known marine biologist in Honolulu, Hawaii, had an opportunity to study this jaw. After a careful examination of the teeth he determined the size of the shark to have been about sixteen and a half feet. Either the original account was an error, or it was an exaggeration (not entirely unheard of in journalism). Most individuals of this species observed or captured are twelve to sixteen feet in length, with reports of twenty-one to twenty-five foot catches reliably given by commercial long-line fishermen. Considerable growth is attained before these sharks reach maturity, perhaps twelve to fourteen feet. Adults will exceed five thousand pounds in weight; an individual of 21 feet may weigh three tons or more. It has been suggested that after a Great White shark reaches 10 feet, add 1,000 pounds of weight for every additional foot of growth. This would seem to be a little much;

Fig. 25. Great White Shark—Taken off Scripps Institute in California. Photos by Leighton R. Taylor. Inserts: (left to right) Complete jaw; Side view of head. Left insert photo by the author.

200 pounds per foot would appear to be more likely.* It would appear that fully grown adults may easily exceed four or five tons in weight.

Reproduction   Very little is known about the breeding and reproduction capabilities of this species. As maturity is reached at a considerable size, very few sexually mature specimens are captured and examined. Most of the larger individuals

---

* The following list of Great Whites taken by rod and reel on various test lines, from both current and past records of the IGFA clearly shows the weight versus length growth pattern for this species:

weight	length	girth	caught by	test line (lbs.)
66	5′10″	28″	Dr. Phil Corboy, Mexico, 10/26/51	12
369	9′ 3″	57″	Mrs. Robert Dyer, Australia, 7/6/57	20
801	11′ 3″	75″	Mrs. Robert Dyer, Australia, 6/11/57	50
912	11′11″	71½″	Mrs. Robert Dyer, Australia, 8/29/54	80
1,068	12′ 6″	77″	Mr. Robert Dyer, Australia, 6/18/57	20
1,053	12′ 8″	68″	Mr. Robert Dyer, Australia, 6/13/57	30
1,876	15′ 6″	101½″	Mr. Robert Dyer, Australia, 8/6/55	50
2,071	15′ 9″	98″	J. Veitch, Australia, 1/9/52	80
2,664	16′10″	114″	Alfred Dean, Australia, 4/21/59	130

The figures for the last two sharks show a weight increase of 593 pounds for an increase in length of only thirteen inches.

The difference in weight between the present record of the 2,664 pound Great White and the recent unofficial catch by Mr. Clive Green of 3,388 is difficult to explain. As females of this species tend to produce two offspring or less, which weigh about fifty pounds at birth, pregnancy cannot by itself account for this weight difference of 724 pounds. It must be assumed that the female was pregnant, well-fed, and simply a larger more robust-bodied individual. It is possible that the differences in weight are due to the fact that many large White sharks are not actually weighed on a scale. Because most scales are not capable of measuring the tremendous weights of these sharks, the proud angler computes the weight mathematically with a formula (see Whale shark).

examined are immature males or non-gravid females. The smallest, free-swimming specimens captured have been five feet or slightly less (smallest known was 4'3" and weighed 36 pounds), which suggests that the young are born at about this length. Based on the size of the young at birth, gravid females most likely produce no more than two puppies (one from each uterus) per litter. The newborn puppies may weigh between thirty-five and fifty pounds at birth.

Diet The feeding habit of this shark equals or surpasses that of the Tiger shark *(Galeocerdo cuvier)*, which is known for its cannibalistic and unsavory feeding activities. When hungry, and it apparently is seldom not hungry, it will readily accept almost anything that presents itself. Various stomachs examined have contained the following items: other sharks (whole or parts) up to seven feet in length, one hundred pound sea lions (a favorite prey), various fishes, sea turtles, portions of whales, dogs, sheep, pigs, horse flesh (in one case reported, a whole horse), both whole and parts of human beings; also much of man's trash and garbage.

Range Once considered to be strictly pelagic, it is now known to be littoral as well. This species is encountered by fishermen in the open ocean as well as by surfers in white water. This shark may very well be attracted closer to shore when following or in pursuit of whales (see "Field Observations"), seals, sea lions or porpoises. Individuals are often observed or encountered in shallow rivers, creeks, and streams, both brackish and fresh water. Its occurrence was once believed to be restricted to the warmer waters; that belief has changed in recent times to include much colder water. The following areas have reported the presence of this species; Maine, Massachusetts, Nova Scotia, Florida, New Jersey, New Foundland, California, Washington, Australia, New Zealand, Hawaiian Islands, and elsewhere throughout both the Atlantic and Pacific Oceans; the occurrences in the colder latitudes take place in the warmer months.

Danger rating **Extremely dangerous,** an unusually aggressive species, with great power and deadly predictability of character. With little doubt, this species rates the highest among the family of sharks for sheer meanness, aggressive nature, killer instinct, and a deliberate purpose for carrying out death and destruction. In attacks, this species has been reported to have approached the victims head on in a straight line, not employing the circling patterns displayed by most sharks. If one or more of these sharks are known, or suspected to be present in an area where you intend to be swimming or diving, avoid the area. If you are pleasure-boating in a relatively small craft, especially those of under 50-foot in size and constructed of wood or fibre-glass, consider this: the motion picture "Jaws" was not just some more Hollywood exaggeration. That movie was based in part on many actual authenticated attacks on both boats and the occupants; many of which were either destroyed or seriously damaged.

Economic importance Recently this species was depicted as the central character in the best seller "Jaws" by Peter Benchley. The book, in turn, generated a motion picture of the same name. The movie was an immediate box office success; a sequel, "Jaws II", was released which apparently had sufficient box office success that they are now starting to film "Jaws III". The original "Jaws" grossed somewhere in excess of $200,000,000.

This species often causes severe damage and destruction to both the catch and gear of commercial fishermen. Due to this shark's habit of intentionally attacking boats, many craft have been lost or seriously damaged.

This shark is recognized by the International Game Fish Association as a game fish.

The present world record** for the largest (heaviest) fish caught on rod and reel is this shark; the record to date is, 2,664 pounds, its length was 16 feet 10 inches, with a girth of 9 feet 6 inches. It was caught by Alfred Dean at Ceduna, South Australia on April 21, 1959, on 130 pound test line.

Related species   None known. The following members comprise this family of dangerous sharks: the Great White *Carcharodon carcharias,* which is the only member of its genus, the Mako shark *Isurus oxyrinchus* (see Mako shark, Related species), the Mackerel, or Porbeagle sharks *Lamna nasus* and *Lamna ditropos.* At the present time this family requires much more study to clarify the confusion that exists about the Mako sharks.

Physical features peculiar to this species
1. The caudal fin is symmetrical (crescent-shaped).
2. The snout is extremely pointed, anvil-shaped.
3. The second dorsal fin is very small, almost inconspicuous, and forward of the anal fin.
4. A round, oval black spot is often apparent on the side of the body near the axil of the pectoral fins (prominent on smaller individuals, weak or absent on larger adults).
5. The teeth are unique in this family; its teeth are similar in both jaws, large and broadly triangular with large coarse serrated edges.
6. The body is usually robust, heavy-bodied.
7. A prominent keel is present on both sides of the caudal peduncle.
8. The gill-slits are very large.
9. The first dorsal fin origin is at or slightly forward of the pectoral fin's shoulder.
10. The eyes are without nictitating membranes, spiracles are absent or very minute.

3-2 Short-Finned Mako Shark
Isurus oxyrinchus (Muller and Henle), 1841
Also known as Mako, Blue-Pointer, Blue,
Bonito, and Sharp-nosed Mackerel shark

Most prominent features   The caudal fin is nearly symmetrical, the snout is sharply pointed.

Color   In life, this species is strikingly blue or indigo-blue above; the undersides are clean white.

**This record has remained the world record since 1959, the fish was caught in accordance with all the rules and regulations put down by the International Game Fish Association. One such rule pertains to the type of bait. The bait recognized by the IGFA for sharks is any kind of fish, this is quite explicit. Any catch that is reported that was taken on mammal bait, land or sea mammals, such as; whale, porpoise, seals, sea lions, cow, horse etc., is immediately disqualified. A good example of the consequences of non-compliance follows. On April 26, 1976 at Albany, Australia the world's largest fish ever taken on rod and reel was caught by Mr. Clive Green. This fish, was a mammoth Great White or as they call it in Australia a White Pointer, it weighed 3,388 pounds and was sixteen feet in length. Mr. Green had used an oversized fiberglass rod and 130 pound test line, unfortunately the bait was *whale meat.* Though this is by far the largest (heaviest) Great White shark ever caught in this manner, neither the IGFA or the Guinness Book of World Records will recognize it due to the violation cited. It might be worthy to note that the present record is 16'10" in length and only 2,664 pounds as compared to this one of 16' and 3,388 pounds, as this one was a female it is possible the difference in weight could be attributed to the fact she may have been gravid. Females of most species of sharks tend to be larger and heavier than most males.

Fig. 26. Short-Finned Mako Shark—11'3" taken off McGregor Point Maui, Hawaii in 120' of water (Aug. 1976) aboard the research vessel "Easy Rider".

Inserts: (left to right) Complete jaw; Close-up of upper jaws center teeth.

Size This species will easily attain twelve feet in total length, some individuals of thirteen feet are likely. Mature individuals of six to eight feet are common. Fully grown adults can easily exceed 1,000 pounds in weight.

Reproduction Fertilization is internal; the relatively large size of the young at birth suggests gravid females may contain small litters of ten or fewer embryos. The gestation period is uncertain, however about twelve months would seem likely. While in the uterus the young will often devour the unfertilized eggs.

Diet Due to its fast swimming ability and aggressiveness, this species is capable of easily preying on large, fast moving pelagic fish such as tuna and swordfish. It may also include both whales and porpoises especially when they are injured, sick or dying, as well as squids, flying fishes, even an occasional sea-bird. Known to include man as well; this fact is borne out by the accounts of many survivors of air and sea disasters.

Range Almost entirely pelagic, however some individuals will enter shallower coastal waters in pursuit of food or while following schools of fish. This shark is often observed in large schools or congregations far out at sea. The specimen shown in Fig. 26 was captured near McGregor Point off the Island of Maui, Hawaii in 1976. This individual, 11 foot 3½ inches in length, was taken in water only 20 fathoms in depth (120 feet) during the last program in which the author participated. Known from both the Atlantic and Pacific coasts of America, throughout the Pacific, including the Hawaiian Islands and most other warmer waters of the world.

Danger rating *Extremely dangerous:* Very similar in disposition to its close cousin, the Great White *(Carcharodon carcharias).* Known to attack boats repeatedly, especially small boats, intentionally and deliberately. There are some authenticated accounts of this species actually boarding small boats and rafts, grabbing an occupant and pulling the victim into the water.

43

Economic importance   The flesh of this species is considered by many to be the most palatable of all sharks, with the possible exception of the Thresher sharks (family ALOPIIDAE). The uniquely shaped teeth are used for the manufacture of jewelry. Often responsible for considerable damage and destruction to both the catch and the gear of commercial long-line fishermen. This species is recognized by the International Game Fish Association as a game fish. The present world record is 1,061 pounds, its length was 12 feet 2 inches, with a girth of 6 feet 7½ inches. It was caught by J. B. Penwarden at Mayor Island, New Zealand 17 Feb 1970, on 130 pound test line.

Related species   Several; this family is comprised of the following members, *Isurus oxyrinchus, I. glaucus, I. paucus, I. tigris, I. africanus, I. guentheri, Lamna nasus, L. ditropis,* and *Carcharodon carcharias.* Of these, the latter three can be eliminated as they are separate and distinct species. The genus Isurus is at present in need of further study, as you can see there are six species shown for this genus. Recently it has been decided that both the Atlantic Mako *Isurus oxyrinchus* and the Pacific Mako *Isurus glaucus* are in fact the same shark. On this decision *I. glaucus* is dropped as a separate species, and *I. oxyrinchus* becomes the single generic representative of the two species. Likewise, *I. tigris, I. africanus,* and *I. guentheri* are all considered to be the same as *I. oxyrinchus* except for slight developmental differences and in time will also be clearly designated as separate distinct species or become synonymous with *I. oxyrinchus.* To add to this confusion, a second Pacific species is now recognized, *Isurus paucus* the Long-Finned Mako. This is separable from *I. oxyrinchus* by its much longer pectoral fins and the presence of blotches or spots on the undersides (usually present on specimens over five feet). This latter feature should not be confused with *Lamna ditropis,* one of the Mackerel sharks also found in this family. The species *I. oxyrinchus* was originally described by Rafinesque, 1810.

Physical features peculiar to this species
1. The caudal fin is nearly symmetrical (crescent-shaped).
2. A primary keel is present on both sides of the peduncle (trunk).
3. The snout is sharply pointed.
4. The pectoral fins are relatively short, with their origin at or behind the fifth gill-slit.
5. The first dorsal fin origin is well behind the pectoral fins' trailing edges.
6. The second dorsal fin is very small and inconspicuous.
7. The trunk (peduncle) is flattened (compressed) both dorsally and ventrally.
8. The teeth are very diagnostic in shape, the central teeth of both jaws are fang-like, with no serrated edges or secondary cusps, the remaining teeth are progressively triangular.
9. The eyes are without a nictitating membrane, spiracles are absent or very minute.

Family PSEUDOTRIAKIDAE—4

4-1 False Cat Shark
Pseudotriakis acrages (Jordan and Snyder), 1904
Also known as Dumb shark or Oshizame (Japanese)

Most prominent feature   The first dorsal fin is greatly expanded horizontally with very little vertical height (eel-like), about equal to the caudal fin in length.

Color   Various shades of gray and brown, dark-gray, brownish-gray, brown slate-gray, even silvery-gray above; the undersides are usually paler shades of the upper body.

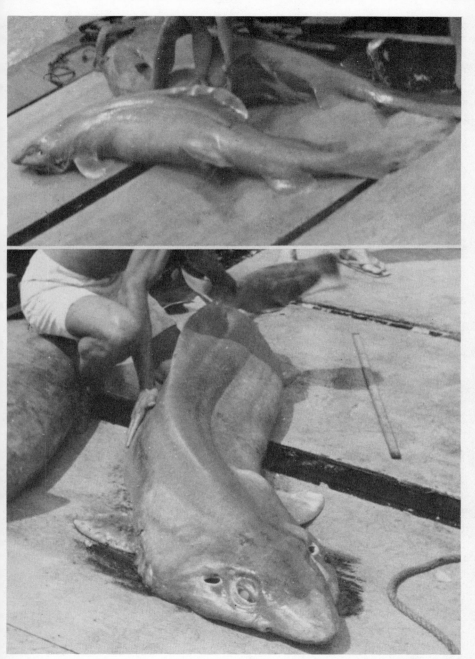

Fig. 27. False Cat Shark—Taken on the bottom at a depth of 1200' off Oahu, Hawaii, aboard the fishing sampan "Alika" during the 1967–1969 Co-operative Shark Research and Control Program.

Size   Based on the sizes of the few specimens observed, lengths of ten feet would be maximum. The author witnessed the capture of two individuals in 1968 both of which were about seven feet. Sexual maturity is attained between five to seven feet. One gravid female of nine feet was said to have contained two embryos. Some fully grown adults may exceed three hundred pounds in weight.

Reproduction   Fertilization takes place internally; this species may produce small litters of six or less embryos. The young are born alive and free swimming. The size of the puppies at birth is uncertain. Little information concerning the gestation period and other breeding habits is known.

Diet   The shape and size of the teeth suggest a regular diet of crustacea (crabs, lobsters, etc.). Its food requirement may be supplemented with small fishes, eels, octopuses, squids as well as other readily available forms of smaller bottom dwelling marine life.

Range   This species appears to be almost entirely bottom oriented, occurring at depths of one hundred fathoms (600 feet) to perhaps eight hundred fathoms (4,800 feet) or more. As fewer than two dozen specimens have been observed world-wide it is considered to be a rare shark. This rarity may only be due to its deep water habitation, and not any population deficiency. It is known to have occurred in the Atlantic off the northeastern United States, North Atlantic off Iceland, Ireland, Cape Verde Islands, Portugal, the central Pacific off the Hawaiian Islands, and in the Western Pacific off Japan. Extensive deep water fishing on the bottom, on a world-wide scale, would probably increase the occurrence as well as the knowledge of this interesting shark. It may be deep-water oriented due to a preference or requirement for colder water temperature.

Danger rating   Due to its deep-water, bottom-dwelling nature it presents no threat to man.

Economic importance   None. Of no interest to commercial or sport fishermen. If one or more individuals are captured by commercial fishermen it may bring some monetary gain from the marine biology department of a local College or University.

Related species   One, *Pseudotriakis microdon* the Atlantic False Cat shark. It doesn't appear to be quite clear at the present time whether the two species are distinct and separable or just wide-ranging representatives of the same.

Physical features peculiar to this species.
1. The first dorsal fin is long and low (eel-like).
2. Large functional spiracles (openings behind the eyes) are present.
3. The eyes are emerald green and oval shaped.
4. The snout is short with rounded broad tip, head somewhat compressed, being ray-like in appearance.
5. The pectoral fins are short and relatively small.
6. The lower lobe of the caudal fin is weakly defined or absent.
7. The lateral line appears as a groove or depression and runs along the latter two-thirds of the body.
8. The eyes are without a nictitating membrane.

Fig. 28. Six-Gilled Shark—Photo courtesy of Hawaii Division of Fish and Game.
Inserts: (left to right) Upper teeth; Complete jaw; Lower teeth. Insert photos by the author.

Family HEXANCHIDAE—5

5-1 Six-Gilled Shark
Hexanchus griseus (Bonnaterre), 1788
Also known as Mud, Gray, Cow, Shovel-nosed, Combed-Toothed
Bulldog, Blunt-nosed shark

Most prominent feature   There are six gill-slits present.

Color   Specimens often display varied shades of gray with hues of reddish-brown to reddish-gray above; fading to dirty-white or paler shades of the upper-body color below.

Size   One specimen taken in England reportedly measured twenty-six feet in length. Total lengths of thirty feet have been suggested for fully grown adults. Most captured specimens average ten to fifteen feet. The larger size reported for this species would indicate that sexual maturity may occur between seven to ten feet. If we accept the lengths of twenty to thirty feet, then individuals in excess of 1300 pounds will occur.

Reproduction   The eggs of the females are fertilized internally; a prolific species, females may bear from forty to one hundred or more embryos in one litter. The young are sixteen to twenty-six inches at birth. The gestation period for this shark is uncertain.

Diet   It appears to be predominantly a bottom feeder; its foraging habits would include various bottom dwelling forms, such as eels, sting-rays, crustacea (crabs, lobsters, etc.), and bottom feeding fishes. The stomach examinations of some specimens captured in Hawaiian waters showed that small sharks (the Spiny Dogfish, *Squalus blainvillei*) are often preyed upon by this species.

Range   It is predominantly a deep-water, bottom-dwelling shark, however, this may be due to a physiological requirement for colder water temperatures. This seems to be

47

evident because specimens are known to occur on the surface in shallow water along the coast of Ireland. The occurrences of this shark in the central Pacific off the Hawaiian Islands is always at depths of one hundred fathoms (600 feet) or greater. In Hawaii at least, the range is limited to 100 fathoms or greater as the water temperature at that depth meets its requirement. This same colder water preference seems to affect three other Hawaiian species that frequently are taken along with Six-Gilled sharks; Cooke's shark *(Echinorhinus cookei)*, False Cat shark *(Pseudotriakis acrages)*, and the Spiny Dogfish shark *(Squalus blainvillei)*. During the day it is thought this species may become inactive, even dormant. This species or a very similar one probably occurs in most oceans of the world.

Danger rating   This shark represents no threat to man due to its usual deep water habit. It may also be an extremely sluggish species. The author was present during the capture of one which measured about ten feet, it was hooked just barely in the lower lip with a #6 hook, on ¼" polypropoline line. If confronted in shallow water it would certainly be a threat due to its size, and very capable teeth.

Economic importance   The flesh is considered an excellent food in some areas. The teeth of this shark are unique, especially the lower ones; they could be used for the manufacture of a unique line of shark tooth jewelry. In areas where this shark is abundant fishermen may consider it a nuisance fish. This species is not recognized by the International Game Fish Association as a game fish.

Related species   One known, the Pacific west coast species *Hexanchus corinum;* the two sharks at present are separated by slight differences in the lower teeth. This family of unusual sharks is usually comprised of the two species shown above, however, due to similar body features and the presence of more than five gill-slits two other genera are often placed in this family. These are the Seven-Gilled sharks, formerly *Notorynchus maculatum (N. maculatus)*, recently renamed *N. cepedianus*, the Broad-Snouted Seven-Gilled shark and *Heptranchias perlo* the Sharp-Snouted Seven-Gilled shark. The Broad-Snouted Seven-Gilled shark may exceed ten feet in length, while the Sharp-Snouted Seven-Gilled shark may not reach more than seven feet when fully grown. All the members of this group possess only one dorsal fin, which is located well to the rear.

Physical features peculiar to this species.
1. There are six, rather than the normal five gill-slits present.
2. Only one dorsal fin is present, and is located well to the rear.
3. The lower lobe of the caudal fin is weakly defined.
4. The eyes are emerald green and oval shaped.
5. Small spiracles are present.
6. A slight groove or depression runs along both sides of the body (part of the sensory system).
7. The eyes are without a nictitating membrane.

Family ODONTASPIDAE—6

6-1 Sand Shark
Odontaspis taurus (Rafinesque), 1810
Also known as Sand Tiger, Spanish, Ragged-Tooth shark

Most prominent feature   Both dorsal fins triangular, the second dorsal nearly as large as the first; the teeth are extremely diagnostic.

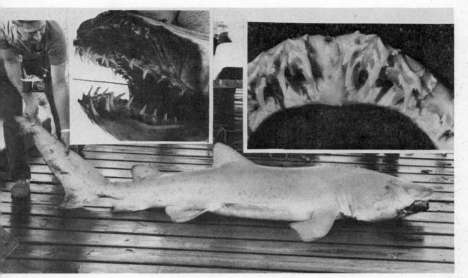

Fig. 29. Sand Shark—Taken off the Big Indian Rocks Pier, Indian Rocks Beach, Florida 1976 by shark angler John Campbell.
Inserts: (left to right) Close-up view of mouth; Close-up of upper jaw (note the fourth small tooth right of center).

Color Various shades of gray, light gray, grayish-brown even grayish-white, above; undersides are grayish-white or white. The body is sparsely spotted with circular, or irregular, dark spots which are often yellowish-brown.

Size Known to attain ten feet in total length; some may exceed this length. Most individuals observed are usually seven to nine feet. Maturity is reached between seven and eight feet.

Reproduction Gravid females have been known to contain several eggs. It is often suggested that this species may begin a cannibalistic nature while in the uterus. The strongest embryo is said to devour the other eggs in the uterus; due to this activity no more than two fully developed puppies are born per litter. However, the author has no first hand knowledge to deny or support this bizarre activity. Fertilization is internal, the young are born alive and free swimming and are about eighteen to twenty inches in length.

Diet Includes small schooling fishes, eels, crustacea (crabs, lobsters, etc.), even small sharks. Larger fishes are seldom found in the stomachs of specimens examined. It is said this shark uses its stomach for more than just a depository for food.*

Range This species seems to be entirely littoral, and they are found in large schools lying on or near the bottom in water only two to six fathoms (12 to 36 feet) in depth. Occurs in the Atlantic from Massachusetts to Florida; the Gulf of Mexico occurrences seem to be limited to the west coast of Florida. The only known capture

---

* The Sand shark, it is said, is able to use its stomach as a sort of swim-bladder. It accomplishes this by swallowing air which accumulates as an "air-pocket" within the stomach. This adaptation by Sand sharks may be possible with other species. The utilization of the stomach as an air pouch closely simulates the function of swim-bladders in true bony fishes.

of Sand sharks in the Hawaiian Islands took place off the Island of Oahu. A research vessel brought up a net during a mid-water drag in a water depth of one hundred fathoms (600 feet), and in the net was a Sand Tiger shark *Odontaspis ferox*. The next day another drag was done in the same area, and again, upon recovering the net, another Sand Tiger shark was discovered. One of the specimens was seven feet and the other ten feet in length. The teeth shown in Fig. 3 are of the ten foot specimen. This species or similar individuals of this group of sharks may be evident elsewhere throughout the Pacific. The above cited occurrence is based on a personal conversation between the author and Dr. Paul J. Struhsaker.

Danger rating   Based on its large size, ravenous teeth, abundance in shallow waters and the reputation of a close relative, the Grey Nurse shark *Odontaspis arenarius* (see Related species); it should be considered potentially dangerous. In recent times many attacks on man have been attributed to this shark.

Economic importance   At one time the hide was used for leather products. Today it appears to be of no commercial value, except perhaps for the use of the teeth for jewelry products. Of some interest to shark-fishing anglers, who frequently fish for them off piers and from the shore. Not recognized by the International Game Fish Association as a game fish. May be responsible for damage and destruction to the catch and gear of inshore commercial fishing activities.

Related species   At the present time this family is comprised of the following members; *Odontaspis taurus, Odontaspis ferox, Odontaspis arenarius, Odontaspis tricuspidatus,* these being "true" sand sharks. One other species was placed in this family, *Odontaspis kamoharai;* however, it is at present being removed and placed in its own separate family as it differs greatly from this group (see False Sand shark).

Except for some variations in the teeth shape, sizes and the location of certain very small ones, at least two and perhaps three species may in fact be the same, these being, *O. taurus, O. ferox,* and *O. arenarius.*

The teeth shown in Fig. 3 are those of the Hawaiian specimen of *O. ferox;* take particular notice of the group of four very small teeth in either side of the upper jaw (teeth numbers 4-5-6-7). Now compare this with the teeth of the Florida specimen of *O. taurus* shown in Fig. 29. You will see only one very small tooth in position 4 and only an empty space where teeth numbers 5-6-7 are located in the jaw of *O. ferox.* Also, many teeth of both jaws of *O. ferox* will have two secondary basal cusps or spurs (denticles) on either side of the central cusp at the base. *O. taurus,* on the other hand, differs by having only one secondary cusp on either side of the primary cusp. The first tooth either side of the center in the upper jaw of both *O. ferox* and *O. taurus* is much smaller than the next two.

Physical features peculiar to this species.
1. Both dorsal fins are large and triangular, the second nearly as large as the first.
2. Dark circular spots sparsely cover the body from the pectorals to the caudal fin.
3. The pectoral fins are relatively short and wide.
4. The caudal fin is larger and heavier in appearance than with most sharks.
5. The origin of the pectoral fins is at or behind the 5th gill-slits.
6. The first dorsal fin is closer to the pelvic fin than to the pectoral fin.
7. The teeth are extremely diagnostic to this species.
8. The eyes are without a nictitating membrane, minute spiracles are present behind both eyes.

7-1 Common Thresher Shark
Alopias vulpinus (Bonnaterre), 1788
Also known as Thrasher, Swingletail, Fox, Sea Fox,
Whip-Tailed and Long-Tailed shark

Most prominent feature Easily distinguished by the long, exaggerated upper lobe of the caudal fin which is nearly equal to the body in length.

Color This shark presents many colors, ranging from gray, blue, even brown; these various hues may have a metallic luster. The undersides may be mottled with shades of white, gray to green.

Fig. 30. Common Thresher Shark—5'1" taken off the Hawaiian Islands, umbilical scar was still visible.

Size Some members of this family may attain a maximum length of twenty feet. This particular species is one of those to reach that length; however, most specimens observed are much smaller. Sexual maturity is reached at perhaps eight to ten feet in length. Due to the extreme length of this shark's tail, its total weight is mostly body weight, with the tail contributing little to the poundage but nearly half of the footage. Fully grown adults may exceed one thousand pounds in weight.

Reproduction The eggs are fertilized internally; gravid females have perhaps no more than four embryos in a litter, with two being more common. The young are born alive and free swimming, and are about five feet in length; keeping in mind of course that half, or nearly so, is tail.

Diet This interesting group of sharks displays a unique feeding behavior, it uses its very long tail to stun individual prey; or by splashing the water it frightens fish into compact schools. At this time it and other Threshers enter the group of fishes and begin feeding. This shark has been observed using its tail to stun sea-birds resting on the surface. Among the prey of this shark are skipjack, bonito, mackerel, herring, bluefish, sea-birds, squids, flying-fishes and various other fishes that occur in its habitat.

Range Pelagic world-wide; however, it is often observed in shallower coastal waters while in pursuit of schools of fishes. This, or similar species is known from both the eastern and western Atlantic and from the eastern, central and western Pacific. In the

Pacific off the Hawaiian Islands, Japan and the vicinity of Taiwan a second similar species occurs. This one is known as *Alopias pelagicus*. As they are quite similar, distinguishing between them has been difficult. It is often unclear which of the two species are represented in any given area.

Danger rating   This species has never been implicated in unprovoked attacks on man; however, as there are two unauthoritative accounts of Threshers (exact species uncertain) attacking a boat, it could be considered dangerous.

Economic importance   The flesh of this species is considered to be of excellent quality, perhaps the finest of shark meat. This shark is recognized by many commercial net-fishermen as a nuisance fish as it is often found tangled in their nets. This species, *Alopias vulpinus,* is recognized by the International Game Fish Association as a game fish. The present world record on rod and reel is 739 pounds, its length was 8 feet 10 inches, with a girth of 5 feet 8 inches. It was caught by Brian Galvin at Tutukaka, New Zealand in 1975. This record appears in error to the author; the total weight is much too high for a Thresher that measured 8 feet 10 inches (snout to tail). That would leave a body length of between 4 feet 5 inches and 5 feet. After contacting the Florida home office of the International Game Fish Association it was verified to have been an error. The weight of the fish was apparently correct, the error was the total length.

Related species   This family requires more comparative study to ascertain exactly how many species comprise it. At the present time the assumption is six or seven, or as few as three. There appears to be two main groups of species; group one consists of two members whose first dorsal fin origin is much closer to the pectoral fins' trailing edge which places its free rear tip well forward of the origin of the pelvic fin. They have a moderate sized eye; in this first group are *Alopias vulpinus* and *Alopias pelagicus,* and one other species thought to be synonymous, *Alopias caudatus.* The second group includes *Alopias superciliosus* and *Alopias profundus.* This group is separable from group one as their first dorsal fin origin is located well behind the trailing edge of the pectoral fins (which places the free rear tip above or behind the pelvic fin origin), and by their large eyes. The two major species among Threshers appear to be *A. vulpinus* the common or Long-Tailed Thresher, and *A. superciliosus* the Big-Eyed Thresher shark.

Physical features peculiar to this species.
1. The upper lobe of the caudal fin is equal, or nearly so to the length of the body.
2. A small, inconspicuous terminal notch is located at terminal end of the caudal fin's upper lobe.
3. The eyes are moderately large and spherical in shape.
4. A small spiracle is present behind both eyes.
5. The origin of the first dorsal fin is well behind the trailing edge of the pectoral fin, the dorsal's free rear tip is well forward of the pelvic fin origin.
6. The tooth count either side of the center of the upper jaw is twenty to twenty-two, and are similar in both jaws, a small secondary cusp may be present basally on one side of some teeth.
7. The eyes are without a nictitating membrane.

The shark shown in Fig. 31 is an example of *Alopias pelagicus* the Oceanic Thresher. As this species is so similar to *A. vulpinus* the author decided not to treat it here separately, but instead to show it as perhaps as being synonymous with *A. vulpinus.* As mentioned earlier this family requires much more study, after such additional study

52

Fig. 31. Oceanic Thresher Shark 8'6" taken off the north shore of Oahu, Hawaii, 1971.

Inserts: (upper) Right side of jaw; Left side of jaw.

perhaps these two species will receive further clarification. At the present time *A. pelagicus* appears to differ from *A. vulpinus* in that its teeth are strongly oblique toward the rear of the mouth (which creates a nearly continuous cutting edge). Also some teeth of *A. pelagicus* possess two secondary cusps (denticles) one either side of the primary cusp basally. In addition to this the total tooth count of *A. pelagicus* is greater with twenty-four to twenty-six either side of center in both jaws, as compared to twenty to twenty-two for *A. vulpinus*.

Family RHINCODONTIDAE—8

8-1 Whale Shark
Rhincodon typus Smith, 1829

Most prominent feature   The dark body is covered with irregular sized circular white or yellowish spots and lateral bands creating a checker-board pattern.

Color   The background on the upper body is dark gray, often showing hues of reddish to greenish brown; overlaid with a series of circular white or yellowish spots and lateral bands. The undersides are usually white or dirty white.

Size As its common name implies, this species is capable of immense sizes, individuals have been reported to reach sixty or more feet in length. Making this the largest member of modern day sharks. The exact size when maturity is attained is uncertain, lengths of over twenty feet seem likely. So great are the total weights of captured specimens that a formula was devised for accurate estimates of their weight. The formula, according to Dr. E.W. Gudger: length in inches multiplied by square of the girth in inches and divided by 800 gives the weight in pounds. The formula is said to be accurate to within a few ounces. Dr. Gudger spent a lifetime studying Whale sharks, and was of the opinion that 32 feet was the average length of this species, but that some may reach 70 to 75 feet. One specimen, a thirty-two footer, captured in the Arabian Sea, weighed five tons.

Reproduction Little data is available concerning the reproductive cycle of this shark. This is due to the lack of specimens available for comparative studies, as well as the fact that because most individuals mature at such large sizes few sexually active males or females are observed. The only information concerning the development of embryos is limited: the young are formed inside of an egg and this egg is deposited by the mother onto the ocean floor where the egg is anchored or adheres to coral, rocks, sea-weed or some other suitable surface. The embryo continues to develop within its egg case and eventually emerges a mirror-image of the mother it will never know. One female examined in Ceylon, nearly 70 years ago, contained 16 egg cases in one of her oviducts. The assumption that females release their egg cases to the outside environment received some support in 1955 when a Texas Fish and Game employee J. L. Baughman, discovered an egg case intact in 31 fathoms of water. Inside the egg case was a fully formed embryo with all the familiar characteristics of a Whale shark, the casing measured 27 inches long by 16 inches wide. Further study of this interesting species may show it to be fairly prolific with females capable of twenty or more embryos per clutch.

Diet The feeding habits of this shark differ from other sharks, being more akin to true whales in their method of obtaining food. The shark swims constantly through the water with its huge mouth agape taking in large amounts of water as well as plankton, crustaceans, squid, and small fishes such as sardines and anchovies. A raking membrane, or gill rakers, inside the mouth is used to sort out the food items and funnel them to the stomach. The large quantities of water is guided to and forced out the gills. This method of feeding may allow this species to ingest some of man's trash and garbage involuntarily.

Range This species is mostly pelagic, however it is often encountered in the shallow coastal waters. Its occurrence in shallow areas may be attributed to the fact that a shoreline current is rich in plankton, or that it is following large schools of small fishes. Occurs throughout the warmer waters of the world, both the eastern and western coasts of the United States, the central Pacific off the Hawaiian Islands, and the Indian Ocean.

Danger rating This is perhaps one of the most docile sharks. This giant has permitted men to walk upon its back, with no apparent concern. However, it has been noticed that some annoyance is exhibited when the face area is approached or disturbed. There are no authenticated cases of this shark attacking man, though man has often given it reason to. The most serious danger from this shark is due to its slow and sluggish habit of basking on the surface; also, for some reason it seems to

Fig. 32. Whale Shark—Smallest free-swimming Whale shark ever taken. Photo by Leighton R. Taylor.

purposely place itself in the path of oncoming boats and ships. Due to this behavior many vessels and Whale sharks have collided with unfortunate consequences to both. This somewhat apparent preoccupation with sea-going vessels may be due to the desire to use the hulls in an attempt to break loose annoying barnacles from its body. In doing this, besides frightening the boats' occupants, it frequently comes in contact with the moving propellers doing damage to both the vessels as well as itself.

Economic importance　As mentioned earlier, this species can cause severe damage to boats resulting in financial loss. When occurring in large numbers in man's fishing grounds, great amounts of available marketable fish may be consumed, causing considerable financial loss to fishermen. This shark was once used commercially for the manufacture of fertilizer and vitamin-A. Regardless of its great size, this shark is not recognized as a game fish.

Related species　None. It is the only genus and singular member of this family.

Physical features peculiar to this species.
1. The entire body is covered with irregular sized circular white or yellowish spots and lateral bands, creating a checker-board pattern.
2. Three longitudinal lines or ridges of unequal lengths are present on both sides of the body.
3. A very large and wide mouth is located all the way forward, being just under the tip of the snout.
4. The first dorsal fin is located directly over the pelvic fins.
5. The caudal fin is nearly symmetrical in shape.
6. Both nostrils are joined to the mouth by grooves.
7. The eyes are comparatively small.
8. The teeth are numerous, from 3,600 to perhaps 15,000 and very minute (and non-functional).
9. The gill-slits are proportionately large.
10. The eyes are without a nictitating membrane and small spiracles are present.

9-1 Spiny Dogfish Shark
Squalus blainvillei (Risso), 1826
Also known as Dog shark

Most prominent feature   A sharply pointed spine is present in front of both dorsal fins.

Color   Various shades of gray, slate-gray to ash-gray above; grayish-white to white on the undersides.

Size   The average size for this shark is about three feet; some may attain a maximum length of four feet. Sexual maturity will be reached at about two-and-a-half feet. Fully grown adults will weigh less than fifty pounds.

Reproduction   The eggs of females are fertilized internally. Gravid females may bear several embryos per litter, perhaps fewer than ten; exact number uncertain. The young are born alive and free-swimming and will be about six to ten inches in length. The gestation period may exceed one year.

Diet   Feeds primarily on fishes smaller than itself as well as crustaceans (crabs, lobsters, shrimps, etc.), squids, and eels.

Range   Usually occurs on the bottom in deep water, may have a physiological requirement for cooler water. In areas where the water temperature ranges between 43 to 59 degrees at shallower depths, you may find this small shark. This shark occurs in great abundance on the bottom in the relatively cool and shallow water of Puget Sound. In contrast, the only occurrence of this shark in Hawaiian waters is at depths of 100 fathoms (600 feet) or greater. Obviously the shallower waters of the Islands are much too warm (about 73 degrees). This shark occurs in large numbers along both the eastern and western coasts of the United States, Alaskan waters, off the Hawaiian Islands, westward to Japan and off both New Zealand and Australia.

Danger rating   Due to its confinement to deeper water and its small size, it represents no serious threat to man. However, many careless fishermen have been seriously injured by its dorsal spines. These spines are used efficiently and accurately for its defense: when threatened it coils itself up and then springs at its victim. The spines are said to contain a relatively weak poison which has required some victims to remain in bed for two or three days.

Economic importance   During the late 1940's and early 1950's great numbers of this species were caught for their livers which were high in vitamin A content; their bodies were processed into fertilizer. The flesh has often been sold commercially for human consumption and considered very palatable. In some areas where this shark occurs in great abundance, it is considered a nuisance fish, damaging both the catch and the gear of commercial fishermen.

Related species   Several species have been described that closely resemble this shark. Of these, two seem to warrant some comparison; *Squalus acanthias* and *Squalus fernandinus.* The first one, *Squalus acanthias* (Linnaeus, 1758), shares the same common name as *S. blainvillei,* the Spiny Dogfish, and a few of its own, the Piked-dogfish, Skittle-dog, Spur dog, Thorndog, and Codshark. This shark is similar to *S. blainvillei* in appearance except for the presence along both sides of the body of small circular spots, white in color. Also the quill-like spine in front of the second dorsal fin of *S. acanthias* does not reach the apex of the dorsal fin. The second similar

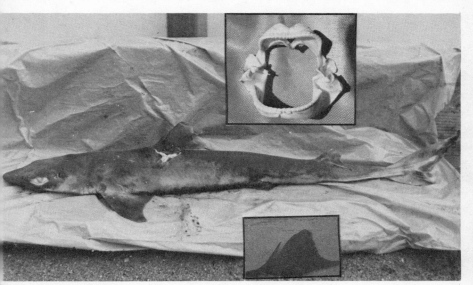

Fig. 33. Spiny Dogfish Shark—Note: white area under first dorsal fin due to a wound. Inserts: (upper) Complete jaw; (lower) First dorsal and dorsal spine.

species, *S. fernandinus* (Molina, 1782) (probably synonymous), can be separated from *S. blainvillei* because the quill-spine of the second dorsal fin is considerably shorter, by about one-third, than that of *S. blainvillei*. This group of sharks comprise part of the family SQUALIDAE. Many are characterized as having spines in front of their dorsal fins, and the absence of an anal fin. One other group of sharks is comprised of individuals that lack an anal fin and, has only one spine, or none at all, DALATII-DAE, the Spineless or Smooth Dogfish family.

Physical features peculiar to this species

1. A quill-spine is present in front of both dorsal fins.
2. The second dorsal fin spine reaches or exceeds the apex of the dorsal.
3. There is no anal fin present.
4. A moderately large and functional spiracle is located behind both eyes.
5. There is no terminal notch present on the upper lobe of the caudal fin.
6. The eyes are blue-green and oval-shaped.
7. A mid-dorsal ridge is present on the midline of the back between both dorsals.
8. A moderate keel is present on both sides of the peduncle.
9. The teeth of both jaws are similar in shape, the central cusps are very oblique.
10. The eyes are without a nictitating membrane.

9-2 Cooke's Shark
Echinorhinus cookei (Pietschmann), 1928
Also known as Prickly shark

Most prominent feature The hide is covered with large, spiny, dermal denti-cles (scales).

Color The coloration of this shark may vary from gray to purplish-brown above; the undersides are paler shades of the upper portions.

Fig. 34. Cooke's Shark—Photo courtesy of Hawaii Division of Fish and Game.
Insert: Close-up of teeth.

Size Some individuals may reach a total length of ten feet; however, most will be from five to eight feet. Sexual maturity is attained between five to seven feet in length. Fully grown adults will exceed two hundred pounds in weight.

Range This species is almost entirely deepwater-oriented: living on or near the bottom. Its usual habitat in warmer, coastal areas is in deeper waters just offshore where the water temperatures are generally below 60 degrees. In other areas where the inshore shallow water has a temperature between about 43 and 59 degrees it can also be found. In the central Pacific, off the Hawaiian Islands, this species seems to be limited to a depth range of one hundred fathoms (600 feet) at its shallow perimeter, to two hundred fathoms (1,200 feet) at which depth some Hawaiian specimens occurred; they no doubt are found much deeper, also. The deep occurrence of this species in Hawaiian waters is obviously due to the average warm (approximately 73° F) inshore water temperature. This shark, or its close cousin *(E. brucus),* is found in the following areas: the east and west coasts of the United States, the central Pacific off the Hawaiian Islands, the western Pacific off Japan, the southern Pacific off both New Zealand and Australia, in the Mediterranean, and off Iceland.

Reproduction As with most sharks, the eggs of the female are fertilized internally. Obviously a prolific species, one gravid female reportedly contained over one hundred embryos (species uncertain). Its fully developed offspring are born alive and free-swimming. Both the gestation period and the size of its young at birth are uncertain.

Diet Being a bottom feeder, its prey include crustaceans (crabs, lobsters, shrimp, etc.), along with various small and large fish, and like other deep bottom dwelling species will frequently consume smaller sharks such as the Spiny Dogfish *Squalus blainvillei.*

Danger rating This species represents no threat to man due to its normal deep water bottom dwelling habit. But if encountered by man within its shallow water range, its size and armament would make it potentially dangerous.

Economic importance At the present time this shark represents no commercial interest to man. Some damage to both the catch and the fishing gear may occur during deepwater fishing activities in areas heavily populated by this shark.

Related species   At least one other species is known, *Echinorhinus brucus* (Bonnaterre), 1788 which is known by several common names, but the most frequently used is, the Bramble shark; the other names are the Spinous, Spiny and the Alligator shark. Both these sharks closely resemble each other in profile; however, *E. brucus* differs from *E. cookei* with its more pronounced and very conspicuous dermal denticles. The two species can be distinguished by the basal (base) size of the denticles; those of *E. brucus* are or slightly exceed about a half an inch in width, while those of *E. cookei* are only about one-third that size or less. These comparisons are based on individuals of six to seven feet in length. The two species discussed here are often found in the family ECHINORINIDAE, however the author has chosen to include them within this family SQUALIDAE as they, like Squaloids, possess no anal fin. One other group of sharks share this characteristic: those found in the family DALATIIDAE, of which some members may have a first dorsal spine but never a second dorsal spine.

Many people familiar with Hawaiian history may feel this shark, Cooke's shark, was named in honor of the first white man to happen upon the Hawaiian Islands, Captain James Cook, the British Sea Captain and Explorer. This belief is entirely wrong; this shark was first described in 1928 by a Dr. Victor Pietschmann from a Hawaiian specimen. Dr. Pietschmann honored Dr. Charles M. Cooke, Jr., of the Bernice P. Bishop Museum in Honolulu, Hawaii by naming it *cookei*.

Physical features peculiar to this species

1. The hide is covered with moderately large, spiny dermal denticles.
2. The two dorsal fins are located well to the rear; both are above the pelvic fins.
3. The lower lobe of the caudal fin is not well-defined.
4. The eyes are green and oval-shaped.
5. A small spiracle is present behind both eyes.
6. A noticeable groove or depression runs along both sides of the body (lateral sensory line), which terminates in the upper lobe of the caudal fin.
7. The snout is broadly pointed as seen from above and below.
8. The pelvic fins are very large.
9. The peduncle or trunk is thick.
10. The teeth are similar in both jaws, with ten to thirteen teeth either side of center in both jaws. Most teeth have three points, two on central cusp, one on the side.
11. The eyes are without a nictitating membrane.

9-3 Cookie-Cutter Shark
Isistius brasiliensis (Quoy and Gaimard), 1824
Also known as
Brazil, Cigar, Plug, Parasite, and Luminescent shark

Most prominent feature   A dark wide band (collar) encircles the body at the gill-slits; the body is somewhat cigar-shaped.

Color   The body is generally brown, with the collar and the upper body darkest; the sides and the belly much paler than the upper body. A vivid, almost ghostly green luminescence is emitted from the body, fins and the head area of captured specimens. The tip areas of both lobes of the caudal fin are much darker than the body area. The margins or trailing edges of both dorsal and pectoral fins are without pigmentation, clear or white.

Size This shark will seldom exceed two feet in length. As with many small sharks of this type, the knowledge concerning their development is limited. This species probably will mature between nine and fourteen inches. Its fully developed offspring may be no larger than three to five inches at birth.

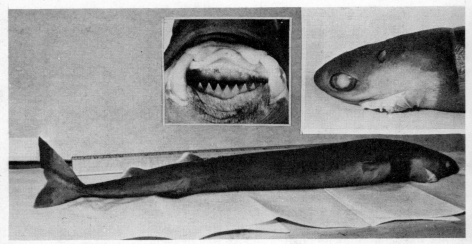

Fig. 35. Cookie-Cutter Shark
    Inserts: (left to right) Close-up of mouth and unusual lip structure; Close-up side view of head, note large spiracle.

Reproduction The eggs of females are fertilized internally; gravid females may produce small litters of up to ten embryos. The young are born alive and free-swimming and are about four inches in length. The period of gestation for this species is uncertain.

Diet The normal prey and feeding habits of similar sized sharks would be expected of this shark as well, such as, various small fishes, squids, etc. However, it has recently been suggested by a Mr. Everet C. Jones, marine biologist at the National Marine Fisheries Service in Honolulu, Hawaii, that this shark has developed a very unique method of feeding. The reader is referred to "Field Observations" Cookie-Cutter shark, *Isistius brasiliensis,* for an account of this strange feeding behavior.

Range This species is a mid-water pelagic shark; it is found entirely in water of considerable depth, both on or near the surface and at great depths. These sharks have never been known to occur in the shallow inshore coastal waters. The presence of this small, and unique shark is known from the central Pacific off the Hawaiian Islands, the southern Pacific off Australia, and no doubt elsewhere throughout the Pacific. It has also been reported in the tropical Atlantic.

Danger rating Considering its small size and its deep water habits, this shark represents no threat to man.

Economic importance None. May be of some value to marine-oriented teaching institutions as a unique, anatomical, research specimen.

Related species None known or described as yet. In general appearance, this shark resembles the smaller Slime shark *Euprotomicrus bispinatus.*

Physical features peculiar to this species

1. A wide, dark band or collar encircles the neck at the gill-slits.
2. A large, prominent spiracle is present behind each eye: nearly on top of the head.
3. The margins or trailing edges of all fins are white or without pigmentation.
4. There is no anal fin present.
5. The snout is wide and blunt with its tip protruding slightly.
6. Both lobes of the caudal fin are about equal in size and shape (rudder-like).
7. Both dorsal fins are well to the rear—the first above, the second behind the pelvic fin.
8. The body is fusiform, somewhat cigar-shaped.
9. The eyes are quite large; the pupils are green.
10. The mouth has very well-developed lips.
11. The teeth of both jaws are dissimilar: the uppers are minute and hook-shaped while the lowers are large and triangular.
12. The eyes are without a nictitating membrane.
13. The gill-slits or clefts are extremely small.

Family ORECTOLOBIDAE—10

10-1 Nurse Shark
Ginglymostoma cirratum (Bonnaterre), 1788

Most prominent feature   The two dorsal fins are quite large, broad and triangular; both are located well to the rear and are nearly equal in size.

Color   The body is generally yellowish to grayish-brown above; slightly paler below. The bodies of smaller, younger individuals will be marked with small, dark, circular spots which fade with growth.

Size   Fully grown adults are capable of attaining fourteen feet in total length. The average size of most individuals observed is between seven to twelve feet. Maturity

Fig. 36   Nurse Shark (Florida specimen)
 Inserts: (left to right) Mouth showing barbles or feelers; Upper jaw; Lower jaw seen from behind, showing many rows of replacement teeth.

61

seems to occur at between five to seven feet in length. Healthy, well nourished adults may reach several hundred pounds in weight; an eight footer could weigh about three hundred and fifty pounds.

Reproduction   The eggs of females are fertilized internally. Initially the young are developed within an egg, and are later hatched in the uteri where they continue to develop via an umbilical cord. A gravid female is capable of bearing some thirty embryos per litter. The young are born alive and free swimming.

Diet   As it is generally a bottom feeder, it has a preference for crustaceans (crabs, lobsters, shrimps etc.), as well as squids, various small fishes, and even sea urchins.

Range   It is an entirely littoral species and its haunts are the shallow to very shallow inshore coastal waters. It would not be uncommon to find one or more of these individuals in water no deeper than two feet. Often, scuba divers encounter this shark on the bottom in large schools of one dozen or more lying inactive. During their breeding season, divers often observe them mating. This species is known to occur from North Carolina to South America, in the Gulf of Mexico, off West Africa, and from southern California to Central America. It is a very common shark throughout the waters of Florida. This shark is not yet known from the central Pacific.

Danger rating   This species is normally very docile. While resting on the bottom they are often approached, even touched by some scuba-divers. Because many divers have safely handled some in this manner, it became somewhat of a sport with many of them—even to the point of riding these sharks. Obviously this species was considered to be a harmless shark (foolishly). With the increased use of scuba gear in the last several years, many more people come in contact with this "docile" shark. Due to this, the number of authenticated cases of both provoked as well as unprovoked attacks has risen to a dozen or more. Apparently this docile, peace loving shark has taken all it's going to from man and is now fighting back—in self-defense.

Economic importance   In Florida, shark fisheries once used its hide for the manufacture of leather products. The flesh is considered tasty, and in the West Indies it is sold in the markets as a good source of protein.

Related species   This family is comprised of some 12 genera and several different species; however, this one is the most common representative of its genus. The relatively docile Nurse shark of North America should not be confused with the Grey Nurse shark *Odontaspis arenarius* of Australia. Unlike the Nurse shark so common in Florida, the Grey Nurse is a well known, vicious man-eater to Australians (refer to Sand shark, *O. taurus*).

Physical features peculiar to this species
1. The two dorsal fins are large, broad, triangular, and are located well to the rear, and are nearly equal in size.
2. The lower lobe of the caudal fin is nearly absent, and weakly developed.
3. The nostrils have fleshy feelers, or barbles, which connect to the mouth by a small groove.
4. The body of a younger, smaller individual is covered by small dark circular spots which fade with growth.
5. The fourth and fifth gill-slits are close together.
6. The snout is broadly rounded as seen from above and below.
7. The teeth are alike in both jaws and very small; the central cusps are lying down, facing inward.
8. The eyes are without nictitating membranes; small spiracles are present behind both eyes.

11 Seldom Encountered Species:
of no consequence to inshore fishermen or swimmers.

11-1 Hawaiian shark
Etmopterus villosus (Gilbert), 1905

Fig. 37. Hawaiian Shark

Only two or three other species are known to be smaller than this shark. Adults will seldom exceed eighteen inches in total length. This shark occurs well off-shore in, water of considerable depth. This small shark is known from the Hawaiian Islands and throughout the warmer waters of the world. The body of this shark may radiate a luminescent glow in the dark.

11-2 Slime shark
Euprotomicrus bispinatus (Quoy and Gaimard), 1824

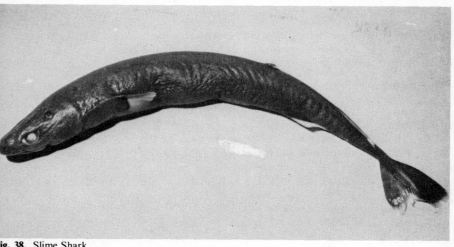

ig. 38. Slime Shark

63

This shark, and one other *(E. laticaudus)* are perhaps the smallest known species to science. Individuals captured have reached twelve inches but as yet, no larger specimen has been observed. Like the Hawaiian shark above, this tiny shark occurs well offshore, over great depths off the Hawaiian Islands and throughout most of the warmer waters of the world. This shark may emit a phosphorescent glow in the dark.

11-3 False Sand shark
Pseudo-Odontaspis kamoharai (Matsubara), 1936

Fig. 39. False Sand Shark
Inserts: (upper left to right) Close-up of mouth, front view; (lower) View of the underside.

A relatively small shark, fully grown adults will seldom exceed three and a half feet in total length. Occurs in open ocean far out at sea off the Hawaiian Islands, and throughout the warmer waters of the world.

12 Field Observations

Carcharhinus milberti The author caught a 6-foot female Sandbar shark off Honolulu, Hawaii on December 27, 1968. She was placed in a large tank at the University of Hawaii's research facility at Kewalo Basin. Both the author and Mr. Richard C. Wass, whom the author was assisting, noted that her girth was somewhat more than normal, indicating she was gravid. Almost nine months to the day, on September 24, 1969, she gave birth, an account of this event follows: September 24, 1969 at 1600 hours—that afternoon Dick Wass and I guided the female, named "Sandy", into a large holding net to administer an anesthetic (MS222) through her gill-slits. She was then placed on her side on a table which we had lowered into the tank. Our original intention was to take body measurements and do a teeth examination. As her girth was considerably greater since her capture, Dick decided to examine her cloacal opening. Upon inserting his finger he felt the tail of an embryo. In doing this, he had apparently ruptured the placenta membrane because as he withdrew his finger fluid drained from the opening. After completing the examination, Dick "walked" her around the tank to flush the anesthetic from her system. After about ten minutes we observed a tail protruding from her cloaca. Dick then pulled the embryo by the tail from the opening and placed it in a smaller separate tank where it began swimming naturally in a few minutes. About 1800 hours that evening, Sandy was observed swimming faster than her normal rate. We observed the tails of two more embryos trailing from the cloaca in unison with the swimming motions of the mother. At 1845 hours a third tail was protruding from the mother's cloaca. At this point Dick entered the tank. The water depth was only about 1 meter (3.28 feet). By now Sandy was swimming about twice her normal speed and making sharp turns. At one point she made a 180 degree turn and had left a puppy at her pivot point. After some twenty minutes the puppy was swimming about the tank normally. The final number of embryos from Sandy's litter totaled eight; of these, four were terminal (meaning ready for birth), the largest measured 26.8 inches in total length which is larger than normal. The other four were stillborn, which is abnormal, and will be discussed later. By 1945 hours Sandy had returned to her normal swimming pattern. The umbilical cords could be seen still trailing from the birth canal. The sex ratio of the entire litter was 1:1, four females and four males. The live pups were measured the next day. One female was 67 cm (26.8 inches) in total length, the pre-caudal measurement (snout to origin of the caudal) was 51.2 cm (20.48 inches). Two others, a female and a male, measured the same 67 cm in total length and 51.0 cm (20.4 inches) in precaudal length. The fourth one was the runt, a male, measuring 63 cm (25.2 inches) total length and with a pre-caudal length of 47.8 cm (19.12 inches). Dick attributed the larger size of these puppies to the conditions of confinement which may have increased their period of pre-natal development. The total lengths of the four stillborn were; male, 33 cm (13.2 inches); male, 33 cm (13.2 inches); female, 32 cm (12.8 inches), and female 32 cm (12.8 inches).

Both the author and Mr. Wass were convinced that the four stillborn pups occurred due to an injury the mother sustained during her capture and handling. We had placed her in a heavy canvas on her right side and lifted her from the water. In this manner we carried her in our arms into the facility. The pregnancy apparently was terminated within the right uterus due to her own body pressing against her uterus and our arms.

The day following the birth Sandy resumed her normal feeding habit. By the fifth day all the puppies were feeding normally. Within three weeks a visible slit on their bellies completely closed leaving a scar. These umbilical scars disappeared entirely at six months of age during which time the pups had added 15.8 centimeters to their total length, a 6.32 inch increase.

Carcharhinus limbatus

Carcharhinus limbatus   During the 1971 Shark Research and Control Program in Hawaii the author was checking a shark that had just been boarded. A dark band was prominent on both sides of the body, all the fins were conspicuously black-tipped and the upper teeth appeared correct in shape. With these features evident, the shark was identified as a Small Black-Tipped *C. limbatus*. If the shark had been disposed of over the side that would have been the end of it, however, the author removed the jaws, to be cleaned later. Upon returning to port the author began cleaning two jaws, both were taken from Small Black-Tipped sharks. While cleaning the jaws the author noticed a slight difference between the two; the upper teeth were somewhat dissimilar in shape. Because of this difference, I realized my error.

During a visit to the west coast of Florida in 1976 the author repeated this same error in identification. I discovered a good source of captured sharks at the Clearwater Municipal Boat Harbor, many charter fishing boats took tourists out on shark fishing trips regularly. One day a charter boat brought in a five or six foot shark, the captain and the proud angler asked me what kind of shark was it. Again the obvious dark band was present on both sides of the body. Its fins were all black-tipped and the teeth seemed correct. This time I took a profile photograph and removed the jaw. I informed the captain and the angler that they had a Small Black-Tipped shark. As I was allowed to retain the jaw, I immediately went to the State Marine Lab facility in St. Petersburg. There under the microscope was the proof; the lower teeth had smooth edges, no serrations, and again another Small Black-Tipped shark became a Large Black-Tipped. The above incidents described are meant to show two things; first, that identification of any shark, and especially these two, are subject to error; and, secondly, that in an area where one of these two species is known, the other species may well be present also.

Carcharhinus limbatus This is an incident related to the author by one scuba-diver; this same story was repeated by other divers as well. "I was on the bottom in fifty to sixty feet of water and had just speared an average sized octopus, when I noticed two sharks approaching very fast. One seemed to be about seven or eight feet, the other about five or six feet in length. Both appeared to be very excited, but showed little concern over my presence, when the larger one began swimming excitedly about me, it became increasingly clear to me that it wanted my octopus. At this point I stretched out my spear, with the octopus impaled on the end, well out from me in an offering gesture to the sharks. The largest one came straight in with its mouth agape and hit the octopus (which was still alive), clamped its jaws over it, and instantly slid it off the end of the spear. As the larger shark swam away with part of the octopus hanging from its mouth, the smaller companion swam along side making attempts to grab portions of the victim from its mouth."

From this account two things are apparent: first, that this species (as with most sharks) becomes excited and dangerous when freshly speared fish (or any marine life) are present; secondly, that, at least in this incident, the sharks obviously preferred the speared octopus over the man. Upon listening to the diver's description of the two sharks in this account, it was very clear to the author that both were Small Black-Tipped sharks.

Isistius brasiliensis The suggested cause of crater wounds on various fishes. The following is based in part on an article from the Fishery Bulletin; Vol. 69, No. 4 by Mr. Everet C. Jones, National Marine Fisheries Service, Fishery Research Center, Honolulu, Hawaii: For many years the presence of strange circular, or crescent shaped wounds have been observed on the bodies of many different pelagic fishes. These wounds, often referred to as "crater wounds", have been seen by scientists, commercial and sport fishermen alike. The wounds have always been attributed to birds (sea-birds) by fishermen and by leeches or lampreys by many scientists.

Speculation as to the causes of these strange, circular sores suggests that this small shark *I. brasiliensis* the Cookie-Cutter, rather than sea-birds is the perpetrator. It may be shown with further study that some wounds of a different nature may be the work of leeches or lampreys.

Mr. Everet C. Jones further speculates as to how this relatively small shark is able to accomplish such a unique method of feeding. This shark's small size suggests it isn't capable of speed sufficient to chase down larger and swifter pelagic fishes. Apparently it uses a cat and mouse behavior. When a school of pelagic fishes or other potential prey appear, this shark may simply wait until they approach his location. At this time he may utilize his luminescence (at night) to attract the passing school to him. At this point its intended prey advance closer to him with the intention of gaining a potential meal. Upon closer examination the fish or fishes realize it isn't a preferred source of food and veer off. It is at this moment that *I. brasiliensis* probably makes its move. With a sudden spurt of speed the little shark dashes forward to its chosen victim. With its mouth agape it impacts upon the body of the fish; its teeth penetrate the skin, the lips are pressed against the skin, and attachment is complete. At this instant, *I. brasiliensis* becomes a parasite, which it will remain, until separation occurs.

The next element required for this unusual behavior is provided by the host. Upon feeling the initial impact as well as the painful bite that ensued, the frightened fish darts off. The fish begins swimming vigorously in an attempt to dislodge its unwanted hitchhiker, in doing so it creates a rush of water along its body. It is this fast moving rush of water that twirls the small shark's body in an arc. If this arc is completed the shark will fall away, and with him a small plug of the fish's flesh is removed. If the shark falls away before the arc is completed than a crescent wound would result.

The following list contains those marine forms often observed with crater wounds on their bodies; skipjack, yellowfin tuna, albacore, wahoo, large jack, dolphin (Coryphaena hippurus), swordfish, rainbow runner, various marlin, beaked whale, sperm whale, baleen whale, and various porpoises.

It is further explained that this parasitic behavior by *I. brasiliensis* is accomplished by the combined use of well-developed lips, a well-developed and movable tongue, and the temporary closing of the large functional spiracles. As a result of the combined use of these three aspects a sufficient vacuum is produced against the smooth body of the fish.

The teeth are very well adapted for this feeding behavior; the upper teeth are extremely small and hook shaped, they provide the guide or the track the lower teeth will follow, while the much larger and triangular lower teeth provide the actual cutting edge.

Carcharodon carcharias   Beached whales, seals, sea lions, or porpoise found decomposing on a beach may attract this predator into the area. Such an area would wisely be avoided by bathers, scuba-divers and surfers. The beach would warrant the posting of "Beach Closed" signs by the authorities for several days following the removal of the carcasses. This would allow the dissipation of any and all traces of the scent, body fluids etc. of the animals that would have certainly remained in the sand. The following is a good example of the above: Early in 1969, at Makaha Beach, on the western shore of Oahu, Hawaii, for three or four days the body of a large whale was allowed to remain on the beach before the authorities had the animal removed. Its presence in no way deterred people from using the beach and the beckoning waters. Shortly after the whale had been disposed of, a young Hawaiian youth in his mid-teens, along with his mini-board entered the water. The boy was out some distance from shore in white-water lying on the board waiting for a good wave. After the attack the boy related the following: "I felt the board being pushed and rocked. My first thought was that one of the other surfers was pushing my board. When I turned to see who it was, I saw no one near me. Just about then I again was pushed sideways in the water. I looked down toward the water and there below me, trying to bite my board, was a large dark fish. During one of the passes the shark made on me and my board, it bit the board in half and its teeth slashed my leg. Somehow in the fright and confusion of the attack I managed to reach the beach, still holding the other half of my board." A couple days later, Mr. Richard C. Wass and I visited with the boy at his home. We lis-

67

tened to his recounting of the attack and his description of the shark. We were also shown the section of his mini-board. In the board you could see the perfect impressions, both top and bottom, of the shark's teeth. Also a complete crescent shape of both the upper and lower jaws was clearly evident on the board. We were shown the wound on his leg which was 5 inches in length and required twenty-three stitches. The teeth and jaw impressions on the board clearly showed that the attacker had large serrated teeth, triangular in shape and similar in both jaws. The physical evidence indicated the shark was large, heavy looking, and dark in color. All of this evidence plus the fact the attack took place in shallow white-water in an area that a few days ago a whale lay decomposing, clearly indicated the predator involved. It was clear the shark responsible in this attack was a Great White of about eleven feet in length. The Great White was almost certainly attracted into the area by the presence of the whale's scent still remaining in the sand and washing out to sea.

Sphyrna lewini This incident was related to the author by a friend, Mr. David Norquist, who is a very active scuba diver in Hawaii.

"This particular time I was diving alone. I was on the bottom in fifty or sixty feet of water collecting various tropical fish which I later sold to tropical fish dealers. Suddenly, I caught a glimpse of some movement at a considerable distance; visibility was much better this day than at other times. I stood there watching this yet indiscernible movement which was still some distance away. It was clear that whatever it may be was heading straight toward me. After what seemed like several minutes, but was really only seconds, I was able to see what it was. My new diving partner was a large shark, to be more precise a Hammerhead shark, and from the shape of its head it was a Scalloped Hammerhead (determined later after our discussion). The shark was between seven and eight feet in length. It continued swimming in my general direction, and this fact concerned me. It was swimming no more than two feet above the sand bottom, swinging its head from side to side. It seemed to be excited, as if it was searching for something. At this point the thought hit me, I hope it's not me it's tracking. At about twenty feet from me it suddenly veered to its left, passing me. The shark seemed to become much more intent, increasing its speed. I looked ahead of the shark's path, and there buried in the sand, with only its eyes and spiracles visible, was an average sized sting-ray. It must have been asleep as it showed no concern of the approaching predator. The Hammerhead was now no more than a foot above the bottom and swimming directly toward the unsuspecting ray. Upon reaching the ray the shark instantly hit it from above with its mouth agape. Immediately the water became cloudy with the stirred up sand from the sudden confrontation. Within the clouded water I got fleeting glimpses of the struggle. Both were rolling and thrashing above the bottom. Suddenly, out of this mayhem, I saw the shark dart off and swiftly disappear. Simultaneously, the somewhat shaken victim emerged and it too swam away, in the opposite direction. As the ray retreated, I could see that a sizeable piece was missing from one of its wings, a crescent shaped wound of perhaps seven or eight inches in diameter was clearly evident."

This account, as in similar cases, again, indicates that sharks when given a choice between familiar prey or man seem to prefer the more familiar of the two.

"The most dangerous shark is the one coming straight at you with its mouth open."

The author

Fig. 40. "Megamouth" The Pacific Large-Mouth Shark, an entirely new family, genus and species, caught off the Island of Oahu, Hawaii 15 November 1976. A scientific paper will soon be completed by Dr. Leighton R. Taylor describing this newest member of the family of sharks. Photos by Mr. Chuck Peterson.

Insert: "Megamouth" as seen from above.

INDEX OF COMMON NAMES

Tiburon Amarillo 29
Tiger 4, 15, 16, 17, 41
Whale 9, 40, 53, 54, 55
Whip-Tailed 51
White 39, 40
White-Death 39

White-Pointer 39, 42
White-Tip 10, 33
White-Tipped Reef 33
Wreck 27
Yellow Shark 29
Zambezi River 25

INDEX OF SCIENTIFIC NAMES

INDEX OF SCIENTIFIC NAMES

Conversion table, standard to metric

1 inch = 2.54 centimeters
.39 inches = 1 centimeter
1 inch = 25.4 millimeters

farenheit to celsius, subtract 32 and multiply by 0.56
celsius to farenheit, multiply by 1.8 then add 32
pounds to kilograms, multiply by 0.45